C000135862

Marseille
& Western
Provence

Tristan Rutherford and Kathryn Tomasetti

Credits

Footprint credits

Editor: Alan Murphy
Production and layout: Jen Haddington
Maps: Gail Townsley

Managing Director: Andy Riddle
Content Director: Patrick Dawson
Publisher: Alan Murphy
Publishing Managers: Felicity Laughton,
Jo Williams, Nicola Gibbs
Marketing and Partnerships Director:
Liz Harper
Marketing Executive: Liz Eyles
Trade Product Manager: Diane McEntee
Account Managers: Paul Bew, Tania Ross
Advertising: Renu Sibal, Elizabeth Taylor
Finance: Phil Walsh

Photography credits
Front cover: Thierry Maffeis/Dreamstime
Back cover: Gynoclub/Dreamstime

Printed in Great Britain by CPI Antony Rowe,
Chippenham, Wiltshire

MIX
Paper from
responsible sources
FSC
www.fsc.org
FSC® C013604

Every effort has been made to ensure that
the facts in this guidebook are accurate.
However, travellers should still obtain advice
from consulates, airlines, etc about travel
and visa requirements before travelling.
The authors and publishers cannot
accept responsibility for any loss, injury or
inconvenience however caused.

Publishing information
Footprint *Focus Marseille & Western Provence*
1st edition
© Footprint Handbooks Ltd
April 2012

ISBN: 978 1 908206 56 5
CIP DATA: A catalogue record for this book is
available from the British Library

® Footprint Handbooks and the Footprint
mark are a registered trademark of Footprint
Handbooks Ltd

Published by Footprints
6 Riverside Court
Lower Bristol Road
Bath BA2 3DZ, UK
T +44 (0)1225 469141
F +44 (0)1225 469461
footprinttravelguides.com

Distributed in the USA by Globe Pequot
Press, Guilford, Connecticut

The content of Footprint *Focus Marseille &
Western Provence* has been extracted from
Footprint's *Provence & Côte d'Azur* which was
researched and written by Tristan Rutherford
and Kathryn Tomasetti.

Contents

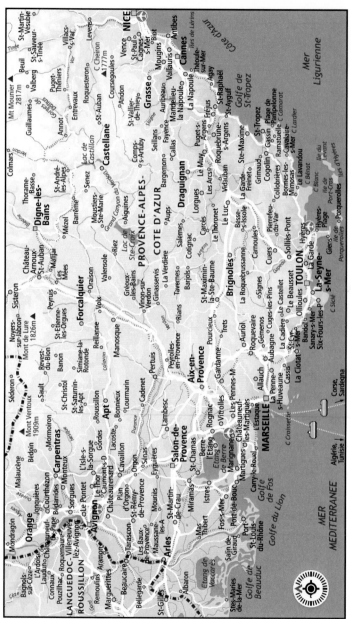

Western Provence conjures up a volley of sun-kissed images. From lavender fields (the Lubéron), Cézanne paintings (Aix-en-Provence) and *French Connection* chase scenes (Marseille) to panoramas of *pétanque* players, hilltop villages and pavement cafés (all three just about anywhere in the region), this region is France at is most beautiful. And for every celebrated shot, there's another cover-shoot portrait waiting to be discovered. Dip your toes into the Calanques's turquoise inlets, ride bareback along the beaches of the Camargue or cheer on the summertime bull races at Arles's Roman Amphithéâtre and you'll see what we mean.

Waves of invaders have claimed a piece of the above for over two millennia, and who can blame them? They may have soaked up more than their share Provence's sun and drank vats of its wine, but in return they left one of the most vibrant cultural legacies in Europe. From the banks of the Rhône to the jagged peaks of the Lubéron mountains, there are more castles, museums, forts, amphitheatres and rococo mansions than most countries possess in their entirety. And with a little dedication, a fair share of these sights can be visited over a single week. Visit once and you'll discover that a year in Provence is a very tempting proposal.

Planning your trip

Places to visit in Marseille and Western Provence

Marseille and the Calanques
A hip urban and appealing rural mix creates this most unique area of Provence. Bookending the region are Marseille and Toulon, two working centres, a blend of ethnic diversity and counter culture. The former is gearing up to become Europe's Capital of Culture in 2013 and has one of France's best music, theatre and 21st-century art scenes. The first part of Provence to be colonised by Greek traders in around 600 BC, Marseille has since welcomed Romans, Jews, Spaniards, North Africans, South Americans and Vietnamese. Between Marseille and Toulon is a region so attractively dated that painter Paul Signac or author Virginia Woolf would probably still recognise it if passing through today. Of the scores of villages in the area, perhaps Cassis and Bandol are the most lovely: wines from these two resorts are the shining stars of the coastal wine industry.

Aix-en-Provence and the Lubéron
The Romans discovered a thermal source in Aix and quickly laid a beautiful settlement on top of it. Locals have been taking care of themselves, and their city, ever since. A former capital of Provence, it's still a staunchly middle-class location, with wide tree-lined boulevards and fountain-filled squares, a far cry from its louche coastal cousins: Marseille, Toulon and Nice. The artist Paul Cézanne was born to a merchant family here in 1839. He's now synonymous with the town, taking inspiration from nearby Mont Ste-Victoire which features in dozens of his landscapes. The clean, green Lubéron countryside surrounds this regional capital, its only harsh edge the yearly *mistral* gales. It would take a year in Provence to fully explore the myriad villages around Gordes and Roussillon. For visitors with just a few days, head to the lavender fields that have made the area famous, starting with those around Abbaye Notre-Dame de Sénanque, where monks still press the purple blossom into oil, soap and liqueurs.

Avignon, Arles and Western Provence
In this region of great contrasts, Avignon stands out as the largest and most orderly city. It owes these attributes to the popes, who relocated here from Rome in 1309, bringing the papacy and all its wealth to Provence. The popes lived in style, as showcased in the must-see Palais des Papes; they also laid out summer châteaux and encouraged vineyards at Châteauneuf-du-Pape. Running southwards, the Rhône forms the western border of Provence, passing through Arles, a gorgeous gastronomic capital that owes its allegiance to a much older Rome. Its amphitheatres and 2000-year-old baths are as renowned as the city's most famous resident, Vincent Van Gogh. From Arles, the Rhône splits and disperses into the Camargue, a salt marsh cowboy country filled with horses, bulls, and flocks of pink flamingos.

Best of Marseille and Western Provence

Cassis and the Calanques Cassis, a pastel-blue fishing village little changed from the 1950s, sits among the Calanques, a series of spectacular limestone cliffs and clear turquoise bays. Try seaside dining, rock-climbing, cliff-diving and touring the local vineyards on foot. Provence at its most picturesque. Page 37.

Cézanne's Aix-en-Provence Step into a Cézanne painting and see where the father of modern art lived and worked. Visit the Jas de Bouffan, where he decorated the walls of the family mansion with a dozen masterpieces, or his final atelier. Then carry on to Mont Ste-Victoire, the landscape that inspired countless Cézanne creations. Page 53.

Lavender The purple lavender-cloaked hills are one of Provence's most enduring symbols. Enthusiasts can hit the Musée de la Lavande, a shrine to the fragrant purple blossom. Or drive deep into the Lubéron to Abbaye Notre-Dame de Sénanque, a 12th-century Cistercian abbey where visitors can buy the monks' home-made lavender oil, soap and honey. Pages 59 and 60.

Palais des Papes For half a century Avignon was the capital of the Holy Roman Empire. Its legacy is a massive Gothic edifice, now a UNESCO World Heritage site, which dominates the medieval walled city. Floor-to-ceiling frescoes, preserved under 500 years of paint and now on display, give an inkling of the pampered papal lifestyle. Page 69.

Château des Baux Balanced on a rocky tip above a medieval village, Château des Baux was a fortified medieval hill town, commanding the countryside and vineyards all the way down to the sea. Expect jaw-dropping panoramas, cliff-edge walks and a collection of larger-than-life siege weaponry. Page 78.

Arles market The capital of the Camargue hosts the region's finest food market every Wednesday and Saturday morning. Stalls selling bull salami, French cheese and the famed local olive oil flank the colourful Old Town. Then step through the city walls to discover Arles's Roman amphitheatre and a volley of amazing restaurants. Page 85.

The Camargue This 1000 sq km triangle of shallow lakes, salt marshes and reed beds supports an exotic array of indigenous wildlife, including the white Camargue horse and pink flamingos. Try riding, kayaking or mountain biking through the vast National Park. Page 87.

Wining and dining Rosé was once dismissed as a rough locals-only drink, but today Provence's tipple of choice is back in vogue. Removing the tannin-rich skins during the winemaking process leaves a soft blush-coloured wine, making rosé the perfect accompaniment to the region's cuisine, in particular Marseille's world-famous *bouillabaisse* fish stew (page 32). Visitors are welcome at most of the beautiful vineyards that cloak the countryside.

Getting to Marseille and Western Provence

Air

There are three airports serving Provence: **Nice Côte d'Azur** ① *nice.aeroport.fr, T08 20 42 33 33*, France's second largest airport, a two-hour drive east of Marseille; **Marseille Provence Airport** ① *mrsairport.com, T04 42 14 14 14*, midway between Marseille and Aix; and little **Toulon-Hyères** ① *toulon-hyeres.aeroport.fr, T08 25 01 83 87*.

From UK and Ireland Nice Côte d'Azur receives over 50 flights a day from nearly 20 airports in the UK and Ireland in summer, and around half that number in winter. **EasyJet** (easyjet.com) has services from Belfast, Bristol, Edinburgh, Liverpool, London Gatwick, London Luton, London Stansted and Newcastle. **BMI British Midland** (flybmi.com) flies to Nice from London Heathrow. **BMIbaby** (bmibaby.com) has flights from Birmingham and East Midlands. **Jet2** (jet2.com) serves Nice from Glasgow, Manchester and Leeds Bradford. **British Airways** (ba.com) has services from London Heathrow and London City. **FlyBe** (flybe.com) has flights from Southampton. From Ireland, **Aer Lingus** (aerlingus.com) has routes from Dublin and Cork, while **Ryanair** (ryanair.com) flies in from Dublin.

    Marseille Provence Airport's hanger-type budget airline terminal, MP2, is linked to Dublin, London Stansted and Edinburgh on **Ryanair**. **Aer Lingus** also plies the route from Dublin. **EasyJet** flies in from London Gatwick and Bristol. **BA** flies to Marseille's main terminal from London Gatwick.

    Toulon-Hyères receives flights from London Stansted on **Ryanair**, and London City on **CityJet**.

From North America **Delta** (delta.com) flies daily from Nice direct to New York.

From rest of Europe There are direct flights from Nice and Marseille to almost every country in Europe and north Africa.

Rail

Rail travel from London St Pancras to any major city in Provence on the high speed **TGV** is a delight. The journey runs under the channel to Paris or Lille on **Eurostar** ① *T08432 186 186, eurostar.com*, then rushes on to Aix-en-Provence, Avignon or Marseille at speeds of up to 300 km/hr. A summer service also runs directly from London to Avignon (journey time six hours). Fares are much cheaper if booked in advance on the Eurostar website all the way through to your local destination in Provence, such as Antibes or Arles. Prices start from around £120 return if booked in advance. Single journeys are sadly not much cheaper.

    If you're planning a cycling holiday and wish to take your own transport there are several ways to carry bikes on Eurostar. They can be folded down and carried in a bike bag free of charge, as luggage. Alternatively, for a £25 fee your bike can be sent as is from London to Paris using Eurostar's registered baggage service, or it can be booked on to the same train on which you're travelling, subject to space (£30 fee).

Road

London to Aix-en-Provence is a 750-km journey, with a drive-time of around 11 hours via Rheims. The motorways are excellent, but drivers will clock up around €80 of tolls on the way. Driving to Marseille takes about the same amount of time; tolls are also similar.

If you're planning a city break, especially along the coast where public transport is world class, then a car will be an unnecessary encumbrance. Direct flights from the UK and Ireland, or train services from London, are normally quicker than driving. Don't forget, you can rent a car in any town in Provence for a few days if necessary.

The National Centre for Traffic Information, **Bison Futé**, website (bison-fute.equipement. gouv.fr) offers drivers current information on all major routes in France in English and in French, including roadworks, accidents and hazardous weather conditions.

Bus/coach Given the speed and affordability of air and rail links, there's really no reason to resort to coach travel. **Eurolines** ① *T08717 818 181, eurolines.co.uk*, does run from London to Avignon, Aix-en-Provence and Marseille; their schedule is fairly inconvenient.

Transport in Marseille and Western Provence

Rail
The rail network in Provence is extensive and efficient. High-speed TGV (*Train à Grande Vitesse*) services link Marseille, Avignon and Aix-en-Provence both with each other and all major points north. Tickets must be reserved in advance from the station, at an SNCF boutique or online (voyages-sncf.com). Standard prices from Nice to Marseille or Aix, for example, are around €28, with journeys taking approximately 2½ hours. Fares for children aged four to 11 are generally half the price of an adult ticket; advance rates for travellers aged 12-25 are often 50% off too, while under-threes travel free.

Most local rail journeys are made on comfortable and affordable TER (ter-sncf.fr) regional trains. No reservation is necessary: just buy a ticket at the station and get on any TER train. A standard journey from Avignon to Arles costs around €7 and takes 20 minutes. During summer, the region's bargain **Carte Bermuda** rail pass (Jul-Sep, €5 per person) is valid for one-day of unlimited travel along the Côte Bleue's calanques, between Marseille and Miramas. Remember, all train passengers on a TER or TGV service must *composter* (validate) their tickets in the yellow machines on the platform before boarding a train.

Bikes travel free on TER services but there are restrictions during rush hours and on some TGV services. Disabled passengers will find wheelchair spaces on most trains (clearly marked on the carriage) – look for the wheelchair symbol on the timetable.

Road
Bicycle The weather makes cycling in and around the towns of Provence a cinch, particularly along the coast or in rural areas. Bike shops are common, as are rental stations. The going rental rate is around €15 per day. The Camargue is flat and great for cycling, as are the fragrant hills of the Lúberon. Aix and Avignon have electronic bike rental stands, and cycle routes spread around the surrounding regions. Marseille, hilly and congested, is not a fun city to bike around. See listings for bike hire details and cycle websites.

Bus The train's cheaper, yet less comfortable, cousin. The frequency of buses in Provence is normally excellent, with a few exceptions in the Lúberon. For trips to towns tucked into the Provençal countryside, they are a necessity.

Car Speed limits on French roads are 130 kph (*autoroutes*), 110 kph (dual carriageways and urban *autoroutes*), 90 kph (single carriageways) and 50 kph (villages and towns) unless stated otherwise. Speed limits drop by 20 kph on motorways and dual carriageways when it's raining. *Péage* motorways are toll routes. Take a ticket on entry and pay by cash or card when you exit a *péage* section. Do not enter the toll lane marked with an orange 't' as these are reserved exclusively for automatic payments under the *télépéage* scheme.

Since October 2008 it has been compulsory to carry one warning triangle and one reflective jacket when driving in France – the jacket must be in the car, not in the boot. The regulations also apply to hire cars, so check that they are present when you collect your car. The regulation is enforced by on-the-spot fines of between €90 and €135. For regulations and advice on driving in France, visit theaa.com

It's generally easy to find parking in smaller towns (except on market days) or along the beach, often for free. In larger towns and cities, street parking is often charged (*payant*) with ticket machines (*horodateurs*) nearby. Expect to pay around €1/hour, and be sure to read the details on the machine, as parking is usually free at lunchtimes and after 1830. The multi-storey car parks in cities issue a ticket on entry. Expect to pay €2-3/hour, depending on the location.

Roads in much of Provence are relatively quiet, and touring on empty countryside lanes is a pleasure. Some routes can get busy however, especially in July and August and particularly along the coast, so set off early or leave the car at home (get the train in and out of Marseille, for example) where appropriate.

Most French drivers are impatient with dawdlers of any nationality, including other French drivers, so don't take it personally. Town centre traffic systems can be confusing but if in doubt just follow Centre Ville or Office de Tourisme signs.

Unleaded (*sans plomb*) petrol (95 and 98 octane), diesel (sometimes labelled *gasoil* or *gazole*) and LPG are available. The SP95-E10 (unleaded 95 octane containing 10% ethanol) is now being sold throughout France. This fuel is not compatible with all vehicles, so check with the manufacturer before use. *Autoroute* service areas charge much more for fuel than French supermarkets. The self-service 24-hour pumps are popular in Provence and accept Visa and Mastercard.

Car hire There are heaps of car hire places dotted around Provence renting everything from a Ferrari to a 50cc scooter. By far the cheapest method is to book a vehicle online before you go (try holidayautos.co.uk, hertz.co.uk or easycar.com) and pick it up at the airport or train station upon arrival.

Foot
Grande Randonnée (ffrandonnee.fr, in French only) or GR walking routes connect most of Provence's historic towns. A *sentier littoral*, or coastal trail, runs almost continuously along the region's Mediterranean shoreline: short portions of the beautiful pathway are easy to access.

Where to stay in Marseille and Western Provence

For a region that's been welcoming holidaymakers for 150 years, the standard of accommodation in Provence is naturally pretty high. The majority of hoteliers are also very proactive. Most staff can find babysitters, recommend restaurants, advise on parking and much else besides: trainee receptionists at a Travelodge on the M6 they are not.

Accommodation standards

Like many countries, France has a star classification system. Ratings are normally very harsh. Some basic no-star options represent good honest value, while hotels in the five-star range represent every luxury known to man. However, it's local tourist authorities who award these ratings, so the system can be a little spurious. Use the hotels in this book, or your own two eyes, as a guide: prospective clients are welcome to peek at the rooms.

Tourist offices, especially inland, are a solid source of local accommodation. Many have lists of local homestays, *gîtes* and mountain refuges. Although the musings of holidaymakers cannot always be trusted, the Tripadvisor (tripadvisor.com) website hosts comments on thousands of hotels, B&Bs, *chambres d'hôtes* and self-catering accommodation in Provence. When exploring a new part of the region, it's advisable to look at the archived features from *The Guardian*, *New York Times*, *Daily Telegraph* or any other travel websites, as the odd little-visited hotel frequently pops up.

Only a very few – mainly city – hotels in the budget category have a shared lavatory in the hall. North American guests may find rooms small by US standards. Most rooms have TVs, although international channels are available only in a handful of high-end hotels: it's assumed that guests would rather be eating or sunbathing than watching the box. About 70% of Provence's hotels have free Wi-Fi.

Self-catering

Perhaps the best value method of holidaying in Provence, especially for families. This is particularly true along the coast where B&B-style *chambres d'hôtes* accommodation is thin on the ground. Self-catering gives you the option of making lunch and dinner: even making breakfast for four people can save €30 a day in hotel charges. Prices for a two-person apartment range from around €250-500 per week, with six-person apartments for around €500-1000 per week.

To find a place it's absolutely necessary to go online. Tourist offices have precious little information on rent-by-the-week apartments and villas, which are often owned by families from northern France, or even Brits, Germans and Swedes. A search on holiday-rentals.co.uk, vrbo.com or holidaylettings.co.uk will distil the best results according to budget, number of rooms or amenities. And if you need Wi-Fi, a pool, or a parking place, you can search for it. French-run Gîtes de France (gites-de-france.com) is recommended for rural accommodation. Be aware, rental accommodation in Provence books up very fast indeed.

Camping

Pitching a tent or parking a mobile home remains extremely popular in France. Sites range from massive commercial ones with swimming pools that attract the same families each year, to tiny, more liberal ones hiding in vineyards by a beach. All have washing machines and good bathroom facilities, while even smaller ones have cute (sometimes incredibly so) cabins to rent, most often by the week in high season.

There are literally hundreds of campsites all over Provence, particularly on the coast. The excellent Camping France (campingfrance.com) website has a list of, and a link to, almost all of them. A pitch for two people will cost an average of €15 per night. Most local tourist offices have a list of every campsite in the area, including prices, facilities and number of pitches.

Price codes

Where to stay

€€€€ over €200   €€€ €100-200

€€ €60-100   € under €60

Prices refer to the cost of two people sharing a double room in the high season.

Restaurants

€€€€ over €40   €€€ €30-40

€€ €20-30   € under €20

Prices refer to the average cost of a two-course meal for one person, with a drink and service and cover charge.

Tight budgets

Budget hostels exist in most cities with beds for around €16 per night including a simple breakfast. Private dorms seem to be friendlier, cheaper, more flexible and much better run than the 15 or so official hostels in Provence, which are sanctioned by Hostelling International (fuaj.org in France). The private options frequently have two, three and four-bed rooms for those travelling as couples or in groups. Travelling off-season, booking in advance and camping are obvious ways in which to slash your budget. Wild camping is not permissible in France, although backpackers have been known to spend the odd night on a quiet beach.

For drivers the scene is positive. Budget motel chains like **Formule1** (hotelformule1. com), **B&B** (hotel-bb.com) and **Etap Hotel** (etaphotel.com) have around 20 hotels each in the region. These clean, basic rooms can be booked for around €35-50 per double. Urbanites can rent an apartment, property or private room from a local through **AirBnB** (airbnb.com); alternatively, try **Couch Surfing** (couchsurfing.com): sleeping over at someone's house in the South of France for nothing.

Food and drink in Marseille and Western Provence

In striking contrast to the French stereotype, Marseille and Western Provence is not a traditional land of plenty. Instead, the region's cuisine is a mix of peasant dishes and Italian influences. Recipes were developed to make the most of harvest gluts, and in times of little to make prized ingredients go the distance. Meats are often used to enhance a dish, rather than taking centre stage, and olive oil, not butter, features in pretty much everything.

Fruit and vegetables are really the local stars, and always have been. Unlike other parts of the world, locals here never lost touch with their traditions. Sure, heirloom vegetables are making a comeback, but you can bet that granny (at her market stall stocking just three seasonal items) never stopped growing them.

Swiss chard (*blettes*) is used in everything from savoury bakes to sweet *tourte*. Courgettes, aubergines and peppers are bathed in a garlic tomato sauce in *ratatouille*. Crunchy raw artichokes, peppers, and even asparagus and broad beans headline in *salade niçoise*. Heralding from the coast but popular throughout the region, local residents favour the same salad in its sandwich version, *pan bagnat*.

Baguettes are a French staple, but the carb of choice varies in Provence. Italian-esque pasta dishes creep in from the southeast, while in the Camargue locally grown rice is a favourite. Sprinkled with *fleur de sel* from the nearby salt beds, of course.

Mer et Terre

Suspended between the mountains and the sea, Provence's traditional dishes encompass fruits of both the land and the sea, as well as more carnivorous offerings.

Surprisingly for this sea-flanked region, not only can fish be a pricey choice, but what you're eating is not always Riviera-sourced: much of the coast has been overfished, particularly in the southeast. *Soupe de poissons* makes the most of the Mediterranean's indigenous rockfish, while *bourride* and Marseille's famous *bouillabaisse* are more high-end options. Slow-cooked or fried *soupions* are a down-to-earth dish, and the lucky will sample springtime *poutine*, tiny fish at their tastiest when served raw, dressed with olive oil and lemon.

If you're self-catering, source your own local *rouget*, *rascasse* and *dorade* at Marseille's morning market in the Vieux Port. You'll often find stalls selling fish and other seafood, particularly urchins, along the quay in every town on the coast.

From the Alpine hills inland, particularly north of the Lúberon around Sisteron, comes Provence's famous lamb. Traditionally, every part of the animal was used, right down to its hooves, a vital ingredient in the Marseillaise dish *pieds et paquets*. Today more mainstream cuts suit our more affluent tastebuds – dishes such as *agneau rôti aux herbes de Provence*. Beef is most commonly found in *daube*, doused in red wine and simmered slowly for hours. There's also plenty of pork, although it's most concentrated in the region's selection of cured *charcuterie*. In Arles and the Camargue, bull is the local speciality, and you'll find it in everything from *taureau tartare* to *saucisson*.

A bountiful harvest

Offered in tiny bowls alongside an aperitif, crushed with capers and anchovies in *tapenade*, pressed to produce oil, olives are a South of France staple. Trees are harvested in the autumn. From November, you'll find market stalls piled high with local mottled green and black olives, both raw (to put up in brine yourself) and already cured. The latest crop of oil will hit shops around the same time. Don't keep your olive oil for longer than a year. Unlike wine, it doesn't mature with age, and should be used (with abandon) from the moment it's pressed.

Drinking etiquette

Tap water is clean and safe throughout the region. If you opt for bottled *eau minérale* instead, note that big brands such as Evian and Perrier can be very pricey. Most locals will order *une carafe d'eau* instead. Coffee is ordered from dawn until bedtime. The milk-heavy *café crème* is only consumed before lunch: order it after a meal and you'll be marked out as a foreigner for sure. Better for digestion is a simple *café* (espresso) or *noisette* (with a dollop of milky foam on top). It's common to sip wine with your midday meal, and a glass is frequently offered as part of a set menu deal. Dinner is often preceded by an *apéritif* – *pastis* is by far the local favourite – and occasionally, you'll be offered a *digestif* on the house when you finish. The French generally relish alcohol consumption, but drunkenness is always a *faux pas*.

Provençal wines

The South of France's climate – sunny, mild and dry – makes for fertile earth and plentiful vines. The region is known for its reds, both light and robust, and rosé wines in particular. Western Provence's premier AOCs include:

Bandol (see page 41) Around 60 vineyards radiate northwards through the valleys around seaside Bandol. Of particular note are their tasty rosés (vinsdebandol.com).

Cassis (see page 37) Another small appellation, sandwiched between Marseille and Bandol. Cassis's 12 vineyards are renowned for their crisp white wines: perfect cool nectar to accompany local sea urchins.

Châteauneuf-du-Pape (see page 71) Strong, pricey, delicious reds, plus a very small percentage of fine – but much lesser-known – whites, produced in vineyards north of Avignon (chateauneuf.com).

Côte de Provence The Riviera's most widespread wine, produced all over, from Marseille to St-Raphaël.

To call or not to call…

If you have your heart set on dining at any of the superb restaurants included in this book, you must call or stop by to reserve a table in advance, particularly during the busy peak season. Don't worry if your French is a little rusty (or even non-existent): most owners and staff will speak some English, and many of the higher-end establishments offer online booking. However limited your language skills may be, remember that *bonjour* and *merci* are always appreciated.

Festivals in Marseille and Western Provence

March
Le Paris-Nice Prestigious eight-stage cycle race passing through Provence (routinely Fayence, Lac de Ste Croix and Manosque) and finishing in Nice in mid-March.

April
Féria de Pâques, Arles *arenes-arles.com.* Easter-time programme of bull fighting.

May
Fête de la Vigne et du Vin (Vine and Wine Festival) *fetedelavigneetduvin. com.* Open cellars and *domaine* tastings throughout France's winegrowing regions on a Saturday in late May.

Le Pèlerinage des Gitans, Stes-Maries-de-la-Mer *saintesmaries.com.* Riotous late May gypsy pilgrimage to parade the statue of their patron saint, Black Sara.

June
Fête de la Musique *fetedelamusique. culture.fr.* Provence-wide street concerts on 21 June to mark the longest day of the year.

Fête de la Mer et des Pêcheurs (Festival of the Sea and Fishermen), Martigues *martigues-tourisme.com.* Late June homage to St Peter, the patron saint of fishermen, with street markets and boat-to-boat jousting near the port.

July
Festival de Lacoste *festivaldelacoste. com.* Month-long opera, music and dance festival in the rarified surroundings of Pierre Cardin's village.

Avignon Off *avignonleoff.com.* Full month of fringe street theatre and music.

Festival d'Avignon *festival-avignon.com.* Fortnight of theatre and art premieres in Avignon's most evocative locations.

Bastille Day (14th) Fireworks and festivities all over France.

Les Suds Arles *suds-arles.com*. Mid-month world music blowout in Roman Arles.

La Marseillaise *petanque.org*. France's biggest *boules* tournament.

Chorégies d'Orange *choregies.asso.fr*. Opera performances inside Orange's awe-inspiring amphitheatre.

Jazz à Toulon *jazzatoulon.com*. The coast's only free jazz festival spanning funk to afro-rock.

August
Les Rencontres d'Arles Photographie *rencontres-arles.com*. Eight-week long photography exhibition in and around 20 historic sites.

Festival de L'Isle-sur-la-Sorgue *oti-delasorgue.fr*. Races between flower-filled boats plus floating markets.

Féria de St-Rémy-de-Provence *saint-remy-de-provence.com*. Parades, agricultural displays and shows of local bulls and horses in the middle weekend of August.

September
Journées du Patrimoine (Local heritage days) *journeesdupatrimoine.culture.fr*. Open house weekend at many of the grandest buildings in Provence.

October
Fiesta des Suds, Marseille *dock-des-suds.org*. Cutting edge late October week of rock-pop-techno-dance concerts.

December
Fête du Millésime, Bandol On the first Sunday of the month, wine producers set up stalls along Bandol's port for this annual wine festival.

Essentials A-Z

Customs and immigration

UK and EU citizens do not require a visa, but will need a valid passport to enter France. You are required to carry a form of identification with you at all times in France, although a photocopy will often suffice. Travellers from outside the EU may need to obtain a standard tourist visa valid for up to 90 days. Apply to the French consulate in your country, addresses on the French Ministry of Foreign Affairs website mfe.org.

Disabled travellers

Tourism sites have improved facilities for disabled visitors over recent years with the installation of ramps, dedicated car parking and toilets with wheelchair access. However, many historic buildings and town centres have uneven surfaces underfoot, lots of gravel and an array of street furniture which can pose difficulties for wheelchair users and partially sighted and blind visitors. Often people with physical disabilities may be disappointed in gaining access to the ground floors and gardens only. Look at the tourist office listings for an indication of accessibility and disabled facilities at individual sites.

Since 2001 the Ministry of Tourism has been working with the industry to develop the Tourisme & Handicap label to communicate reliable, consistent and objective information regarding accessibility to tourist sites and facilities for people with any kind of disability. Look out for the blue and white logo depicting four specific types of disability. The symbols are displayed in airports, other public places and guidebooks to indicate where help is available. Visit tourisme-handicaps.org (in French only) for links to departmental tourism websites and detailed listings of attractions and accommodation that have earned the Tourisme & Handicap label.

Accommodation lists obtainable from the tourist offices (usually available online) indicate which have facilities for the disabled. However, note that this does not indicate a uniform standard of accessibility, and if your requirements are specific, it is important that you check directly with the accommodation provider.

Ticket concessions are often available to disabled visitors and sometimes to their companion, on entry to historic sites. Proof of your entitlement may be required. With regard to parking your vehicle, if you use a disabled parking space, the international blue badge scheme applies. Always display documentation in your vehicle and have proof of entitlement with you if you encounter any problems.

If you intend to travel to Provence by train, Eurostar and SNCF welcome customers with specific needs or who require extra assistance. Raileurope (raileurope.co.uk) strongly recommends that all bookings for access with wheelchairs or assisted access are made through their Customer Call Centre (T08448-484064, Mon to Fri 0800-2100, Sat 0900-1800) where you can get help with rail information, request mobility assistance, and reserve seats and wheelchair spaces. SNCF has an AccessPlus service to help plan your train journey whatever your disability, though it's only in French (T08 90 64 06 50, accessibilite.sncf.com). The regional TER trains have wheelchair spaces on some trains, indicated by a wheelchair symbol on the timetable and again on the relevant carriage.

Emergencies

Ambulance T15, **Police** T17, **Fire Service** T18 if calling from a landline. The European emergency number 112 can be dialled free from any phone, including mobiles and call boxes.

Etiquette

The French are a formal and very courteous society and it is normal to greet everyone you meet. *Bonjour* (*bonsoir* during the evening), followed by *Monsieur*, *Madame*, or for a young single woman, *Mademoiselle* (pronounced *mam'selle*) will start you off on the right foot. At what time *Bonjour* changes to *Bonsoir* is never clear, so you'll occasionally be dismayed to hear a *Bonjour* in response to your cheery *Bonsoir* – and vice-versa. You will usually hear *Bonne journée* or *Bonne soirée* as you leave somewhere. A simple reply would be: *A vous, aussi!* (To you, too!). When meeting someone for the first time people always shake hands, although women often leave this to the men. Even with people you know, such as a waiter at your favourite restaurant, a greeting will start with a crisp handshake.

A *bisou* (a kiss on the cheek) is for good friends and family. It would be highly embarrassing if you initiated kissing someone you had just met, but don't be surprised if this occasionally does occur. The number of *bisous* is normally two, although it varies from region to region and can be as many as four.

Always use the formal 'vous' to say 'you' in French rather than the more intimate form 'tu', which is normally reserved for friends and family. It is best to let the French decide, then you can return the compliment.

Since smoking has been banned in restaurants and cafés, smokers must go outside if they want to light up. Asking people if they wouldn't smoke while you're enjoying your meal *en terrasse* would most likely be ignored. Smoking is not allowed in any public places such as historic sites and tourist attractions. Increasingly, hotels and *chambres d'hôtes* are also making their establishments non-smoking.

You rarely see drunken behaviour in public. Social drinking is generally limited to one or two small beers or an aperitif. When drinking wine with a meal, glasses are never filled to the brim and if you order a bottle, check that the waiter has brought the correct wine before accepting a drop to taste, confirming whether or not it is corked.

Families

Provence, like most regions of France, is extremely family-friendly. Children are welcomed in restaurants with their own menu and, in larger establishments, an outdoor play area. Hotels often have family rooms, or can wheel in an extra cot or bed for a few euros extra. Trains, bus rides, boat trips and sights have reduced fares for under 25s or under 18s, and are normally free for those still of primary school age. While most kids will love to scramble around Roman ruins, National Parks and fairytale hill villages, a major children's activity, be it Aquasplash or an adventure theme park, is never far away from any of the towns listed in this book. Better still, the countless beaches of Provence are clean, fun and mostly long and sandy.

Health

Comprehensive travel and medical insurance is recommended. EU citizens should apply for a free European Health Insurance Card or EHIC (ehic.org.uk), which entitles you to emergency medical treatment on the same terms as French nationals. Note that you will have to pay all charges and prescriptions up front and be reimbursed once you return home. If you develop a minor ailment while on holiday a visit to any pharmacy will allow you to discuss your concerns with highly qualified staff, who can give medical advice and recommend treatment. Outside normal opening hours, the address of the nearest duty pharmacy (*pharmacie de garde*) is displayed in the pharmacy window. The out-of-hours number for a local doctor (*médecin généraliste*) may also be listed.

In a serious emergency, go to the accident and emergency department (*urgences*) at the nearest Centre Hospitalier (numbers listed in the Essentials section at the beginning of each chapter) or call an ambulance (SAMU) by dialling T15.

Insurance
Comprehensive travel and medical insurance is strongly recommended, as the European Health Insurance Card (EHIC) does not cover medical repatriation, ongoing medical treatment or treatment considered to be non-urgent. You should check any exclusions, and ensure that your policy includes cover for any specific activities you wish to undertake. Remember to take your insurance documents with you on holiday – emailing all the details to yourself is a good way to keep the information accessible. Ensure you have adequate insurance when hiring a car and always ask how much excess you are liable for if the vehicle is returned with any damage. It is generally worth paying a little more for collision damage waiver. If driving your own vehicle, contact your insurers before you travel to ensure you are adequately covered, and keep the documents in your vehicle in case you need to prove it.

Money
The French unit of currency is the Euro. ATMs throughout France accept major credit and debit cards. Most ATMs have an English language option or will automatically recognise the country of issue and display instructions in the appropriate language. ATMs inside shops usually levy a charge for cash withdrawals, and will state the amount before you confirm the transaction. Currency exchange is available in some banks, and at airports, train stations and *bureaux de change*. An exchange fee is discretionary. Most restaurants, shops, and tourist attractions accept major credit cards, although restaurants in smaller towns may refuse to take cards and only accept cash. Normally, this will be clearly displayed in the restaurant or on the menu. Toll routes (*péage*) accept Visa, Mastercard and American Express cards but not Maestro or Visa Electron. On remote or minor autoroute exits there are often unmanned toll points which only accept payment by card. Throughout France personal cheques are becoming less welcome as a means of payment. If you require a receipt, ask for *un ticket* (the last 't' is silent).

Costs
Provence is not expensive. A simple *café* or baguette costs around €1, while a good lunch with wine costs approximately €15 wherever you travel. Hotel prices vary greatly depending on the season, but every town in this book has great accommodation options ranging from €60 up to €300. Allow €50 per person per day for a bargain basement holiday, or double that amount for exciting excursions and delicious dinners. Visitors can save by renting an apartment to use as a base and making picnics from the region's many markets.

Discounts
Over-60s and under-18s (and often adults under 25) receive discounts of up to 50% on public transport and museum entrance fees. Don't forget to ask or the reduction may be 'forgotten'. Children under 10 years old can often visit sights, plus travel, for free.

Opening hours
Banks, shops and post offices close for two or more hours at lunch, even if there's a queue of potential customers outside. Restaurant hours are strict: try to arrive between 1200 and 1330 for lunch and after 1900 for dinner. In summer everything

is open, with some tourist-orientated resorts along the coast shutting up from November to March. Many businesses in Provence take a month's annual holiday in November or January.

Police

There are three national police forces in France. The *Police nationale* operate mainly in urban areas and are distinguished by silver buttons on their uniforms. The *Gendarmerie nationale* are under the control of the Ministry of Defence and wear blue uniforms with gold buttons. The *Gendarmes* deal with serious crime on a national level, although tourists most often see them on autoroute patrol, usually riding in pairs on motorcycles. The *Douane* is a civilian customs service whose officers are often seen searching vehicles at autoroute toll booths. It is only these three services who legally have the power of arrest or can issue search warrants. French municipalities may also maintain a *Police municipale*, who have limited powers but deal with traffic issues and enforce by-laws. You may also come across a *garde champêtre* or the *Police rurale* who patrol rural areas and protect the environment. All police in France are armed.

In case of an emergency requiring police attention dial 17, approach any member of the police or visit a police station. If you need to report a theft go to the nearest Gendarmerie who will give you a copy of the resulting report for insurance purposes. Take care of this document, as further copies will not be issued.

Police Nationale offices

Aix-en-Provence 10 av de l'Europe, T04 42 93 97 00.
Avignon bd St Roch, T04 32 40 55 55.
Marseille La Canebière, T04 88 77 58 00.

Post

You can buy stamps (*timbres*) in post offices or over the counter in *tabacs*. A stamp for a postcard will cost a minimum of €0.77. Many post offices now have self-service stamp machines with instructions in several languages, including English.

Safety

Away from very large cities the crime rate in France is generally low. Think carefully, though, about where you park your car at night – and never leave valuables in your car, even for a short time. In provincial towns and cities it is generally safe to walk where you please, although at night avoid wandering into unlit areas. Only carry small amounts of cash, and keep passport, credit cards and cash separate. In restaurants waiters will normally take your card payment at the table, so be suspicious if they take your card elsewhere to process the payment.

Travelling on public transport in Provence is generally very safe. Never leave your luggage unattended at bus or railway stations and always be alert to risk, especially late at night. If you are a victim of theft, report the crime to the police (*Gendarmerie*) immediately as you will need the report (*constat de vol*) to claim on your insurance.

Telephone

French telephone numbers consist of 10 digits and always start with a zero. The area codes are incorporated into the number so the first two digits denote the region (04 in Provence), the second pair is the town, the third pair the district. To call France from abroad dial the international prefix 00 plus 33 (the country code) followed by the phone number required (drop the first 0). Search online for phone numbers using pagesblanches.fr (private numbers) or pagesjaunes.fr (business numbers). For France Télécom directory enquiries dial 118 712 (calls cost a min €1.12) or visit 118712.fr.

Time difference

France uses Central European Time, GMT+1.

Tipping

Many restaurants include service in their prices (*servis inclus* or *compris* is usually stated at the foot of the menu), so leaving extra for a tip is not necessary. In pre-euro years it was the practice to leave about 10-15% as a tip, but in recent years this has declined among French nationals and now it's mostly foreign visitors who tend to leave tips; be aware as a foreigner, this means a tip is often expected. Where service is not included, or where you are happy to leave a little extra for excellent service, there are no rules: 10% is usually appropriate.

Voltage

France functions on a 230V mains supply. Plugs are the standard European two-pin variety, so carry an adaptor if you need to connect your non-French phone-charger or other items.

Tourist information

Incredibly informative tourist offices lie in every town and village and are the best sources for local events, sights and rural accommodation options. Also, try voyages-sncf.com for trains, viamichelin.co.uk for restaurants and france.angloinfo.com for local news and events.

Regional offices

Comité Départemental du Tourisme des Bouches du Rhône 13 rue Roux de Brignoles, Marseille, T04 91 13 84 13, visitprovence.com.
Comité Départemental du Tourisme de Vaucluse 12 rue Collège de la Croix, Avignon, T04 90 80 47 00, provenceguide.com.
Comité Départemental du Tourisme du Gard, 3 rue Cité Foulc, Nimes, T04 66 36 96 30, tourismegard.com.

Contents

Marseille & the Calanques

Marseille and around

A teeming mix of international influences, city chaos and a thriving counter-culture, much of Marseille is exactly what the rest of Western Provence is not: no snoozy afternoons, ambling retirees or seafront promenades here. But for many visitors, this contrast is exactly what makes the city so appealing. Annual urban festivals crowd the city's calendar. There are art galleries and theatre performances by the dozen, a strong music – particularly hip-hop – scene and an innovative culinary tradition: the city claims both *bouillabaisse* and *pastis*, the anis-flavoured aperitif, as its own.

Marseille revels in its appointment as Europe's 2013 Capital of Culture (marseille-provence2013.fr). A driving factor behind the council's unanimous vote is the city's ongoing **Euroméditerranée project** (see page 27). A master plan for Marseille's urban regeneration, it includes the long-awaited **Musée des Civilisations de l'Europe et de la Méditerranée** (MuCEM, see page 28), now partially complete and holding temporary exhibitions in Fort St-Jean, plus a new 3-km seafront esplanade and many other developments.

The non-stop action is not just downtown: during summer, locals hit the city beach, **Plage des Catalans**. True sun-worshippers would do better to head to the stunning western Calanques (see page 37) or south to the **Plage du Prado** seaside park. Near the latter, pretty **Parc Borély**, with its rowing lake, and the **Musée d'Art Contemporain** ① *MAC, 69 av de Haïfa, T04 91 25 01 07, lesartistescontemporains.com/macmarseille.html, Tue-Sun 1100-1700, €3, €1.50 over 65s, under 18s free*, make for great days out.

Vieux Port
① *M1 to 'Vieux Port'.*
It was here (or near enough) that Greeks are said to have dropped anchor and founded the ancient metropolis of Massalia. Today, Marseille's old port remains the city's hub. To the north lies Le Panier, the true Old Town, while La Canebière, Marseille's central but slightly scruffy main drag, runs from the port eastwards to Palais Longchamp. The newly restored rue de la République also radiates out from here, its first few blocks lined with high street chains, its buildings Parisian-sparkly and uplit as the wide road makes straight for place de la Joliette. Bars and restaurants crowd the pedestrian streets that wind their way through the neighbourhood south of the Vieux Port.

The harbour itself is flanked by 17th-century Fort St-Nicolas and Fort St-Jean, and packed with pleasure boats. Frequent ferries (see page 35) run to the Château d'If, Frioul islands – visible on the horizon from the mouth of the port – and the nearby Calanques. As day breaks fishermen drag their catch on to the quai des Belges, setting up stalls for the daily fish market; chefs and locals soon arrive, shopping for local red mullet, rockfish and the makings of *bouillabaisse* (see page 32).

Musée de l'Histoire de Marseille and Jardin des Vestiges (Port Antique)
① *Square Belsunce, Centre Bourse, T04 91 90 42 22. Mon-Sat 1200-1900. €3, €2 over 65s, under 18s free. M1 to 'Vieux Port'. Map: Marseille, D3, p24. Note that both the Musée de l'Histoire de Marseille and Jardin des Vestiges will remain closed until the end of 2012 as they undergo restorations in preparation for Marseille Capital of Culture 2013.*
Accessed via the ground level of the Centre Bourse, traces of the city's ancient Roman port and Greek city walls are contained within the open-air Jardin des Vestiges. Discovered during the shopping centre's construction in 1967, the ruins are complemented by the adjacent Marseille History Museum. Exhibits cover finds from the port, including an ancient merchant vessel discovered in 1974, models of the Greek city and late 19th-century advertisements. There's also a temporary exhibition space dedicated to other aspects of local culture and history, including early 20th-century photographs.

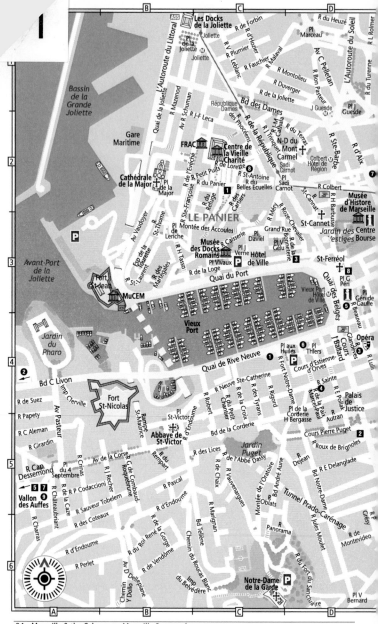

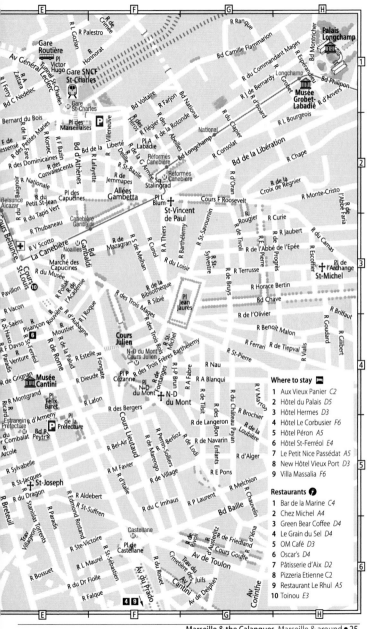

Where to stay 🏠

1. Aux Vieux Panier C2
2. Hôtel du Palais D5
3. Hôtel Hermes D3
4. Hôtel Le Corbusier F6
5. Hôtel Péron A5
6. Hôtel St-Ferréol E4
7. Le Petit Nice Passédat A5
8. New Hôtel Vieux Port D3
9. Villa Massalia F6

Restaurants 🍴

1. Bar de la Marine C4
2. Chez Michel A4
3. Green Bear Coffee D4
4. Le Grain du Sel D4
5. OM Café D3
6. Oscar's D4
7. Pâtisserie d'Aix D2
8. Pizzeria Etienne C2
9. Restaurant Le Rhul A5
10. Toinou E3

Musée Cantini

ⓘ *19 rue Grignan, T04 91 54 77 75, marseille.fr. Jun-Sep Tue-Sun 1100-1800, Oct-May Tue-Sun 1000-1700. Permanent collection €3, €2 over 65s; temporary shows: €5, €3 over 65s; under 18s free. M1 to 'Estrangin-Préfecture'. Map: Marseille, E4, p24.*

Located within a beautiful 17th-century former private home (like much of the city, freshly renovated over the first half of 2012), the Cantini Museum was donated to the city by marble artisan (and creator of the ornate carved statue in place Castellane) Jules Cantini in 1917. Its permanent collection covers the 20th-century masters comprehensively, including works by Paul Signac, Vassily Kandinsky, Fernand Léger, Picasso, Jean Dubuffet and Francis Bacon. Additional major artists of the era are represented in the museum's temporary exhibitions, such as Gustav Klimt, Romanian surrealist Jacques Hérold and German painter Georg Baselitz.

Rue Paradis and rue St-Ferréol

ⓘ *Map: Marseille, p24.*

The heart of Marseille's shopping district, rue Paradis and rue St-Ferréol as well as their many cross streets, are lined with boutiques: high-end brands (Montblanc, Lacoste, Chopard) flank the former, French chain staples (Naf-Naf, Kookai) the latter. There are plenty of one-off shops too. Expect elbow room only on Saturday afternoons. For more shopping in Marseille, see page 34.

Palais Longchamp

ⓘ *Bd Montricher/bd de Longchamp. M1 to 'Cinq-Avenues-Longchamp', bus 81, T2. Map: Marseille, H1, p24.*

An imposing, colonnaded building, Palais Longchamp peers down the long boulevard out front from its perch atop Parc de Longchamp. It took over three decades to construct the ornate Palais; its completion in 1869 marked a glorious celebration of the city's new aqueduct, bringing torrents of drinking water from the Durance River, 80 km inland.

Within one wing of the building, the **Musée d'Histoire Naturelle** ⓘ *T04 91 14 59 50, museum-marseille.org, Tue-Sun 1000-1700, €4, €2 students, over 65/under 21s free*, charts the area's indigenous flora, fauna and fossils, while the other wing is home to the **Musée des Beaux-Arts**, due to open at the end of 2012 after seven years of renovations, just in time for Marseille to take the mantle as Capital of Culture 2013. In the meantime, it's possible to see some of the Beaux-Arts' highlights in other temporary locations around the city, particularly at the **Musée d'Arts Africains, Océaniens et Amérindiens** (see page 27).

Just south of the Palais, the quirky former home **Musée Grobet-Labadié** ⓘ *bd Longchamp, T04 91 62 21 82, marseille.fr, Jun-Sep Tue-Sun 1100-1800, Oct-May Tue-Sun 1000-1700, €3, €2 over 65s, under 18s free*, shows how well-heeled locals of the previous century lived.

Le Panier

ⓘ *Map: Marseille, p24.*

A warren of steeply inclined alleys wind their way over Le Panier, Marseille's original Old Town, located on the north side of the Vieux Port.

Meaning 'the breadbasket' – although the reason behind the name has been attributed to anything from its original market to a popular local restaurant – Le Panier was first settled by Greeks. Over the centuries, these trendsetters have been generally emulated by every wave of immigrants to arrive – from Algerians and Tunisians to Italians and Poles –

each group digging in their heels here first, before earning a little cash and moving on to bigger and better neighbourhoods.

An association with poverty plus incoming immigrants awarded Le Panier an edgy reputation. In 1943, occupying Nazis believed the neighbourhood to be a bastion of Resistance fighters. They gave a 24 hours' notice before bombing half of the district to rubble, parcelling off many of the fleeing residents to labour camps, and the heavy Jewish population to concentration camps. The legacy of this destruction can be seen in the imposing 1950s architecture that swamps the southern side of Le Panier.

Le Panier is still home to a sprinkling of historical sights, including 18th-century **Hôtel Dieu** and **Vieille Charité** (see below). At its western end stands tiny **Eglise St-Laurent**. Around the corner the design for 19th-century **Cathédrale de la Major's** ① *Tue-Sat 1000-1800*, massive edifice was based on that of Istanbul's Hagia Sophia. At the heart of the district, the **Musée des Docks Romains** ① *place Vivaux, T04 91 91 24 62, marseille.fr, Jun-Sep Tue-Sun 1100-1800, Oct-May Tue-Sun 1000-1700, €3, €2 over 65s, under 18s free*, details the city's old Roman dockyards. Atop Le Panier's highest – and windiest – point, pretty **place des Moulins** is now home to just three stone bases of its fifteen 16th-century windmills.

Normally held during the third weekend in June, the annual **Fête du Panier** (fetedupanier.com) sees the neighbourhood fill with concerts, artisan workshops and late-night revellers.

Centre de la Vieille Charité

① *2 rue de la Charité, T04 91 14 58 80, vieille-charite-marseille.org. Tue-Sun Jun-Sep 1100-1800, Oct-May 1000-1700. €3, €2 over 65s, under 18s free. M2 to 'Joliette', bus 55, T2. Map: Marseille, C2, p24.*

Designed by Pierre Puget as a poorhouse during the 17th century, la Vieille Charité came close to condemnation during the mid 20th century. It was only through the ambitious efforts of architect Le Corbusier that the magnificent structure – four pale, arcaded wings around a freestanding chapel – still exists. Today, the centre houses the **Musée d'Archéologie Méditerranéenne**, home to a large ancient Egyptian collection, and the **Musée d'Arts Africains, Océaniens et Amérindiens**, as well as the art house cinema **Le Miroir** and **Regards** bookstore. Note that entry times and prices for temporary exhibitions can vary; entry to the courtyard is free.

Euroméditerranée project

① *Office: 10 place de la Joliette, Atrium 10.3, T04 91 14 45 00, euromediterranee.fr. Mon-Fri 1130-1830. M2 to 'Joliette' and T2. Map: Marseille, p24.*

A huge-scale project to regenerate the city's downtown neighbourhoods, the Euroméditerranée project has been slowly changing the face of Marseille since 1995. All undertaken projects are now finished or works in progress, with the bulk of unfinished tasks due for completion in late 2012, just in time for the city's 2013 European Capital of Culture celebrations.

For a peek at the progress, history of various projects and the city's changing skyline, check out the interactive maps and artists' interpretations on the Euroméditerranée website. The redevelopment is taking place in five main areas, which are spread over 480 urban hectares:

Joliette-Arenc The city's docklands and ferry terminal area. Projects include the **Joliette Docks** (see over page); the **Cœur Méditerranée** (bd de Dunkerque) on the south side of new **place de la Méditerranée**, which includes two hotels (Suite and Ibis); the new **FRAC** (see below); and **M3 Euromed Station-Urban Square**, comprising shops, offices and a retirement home.

St-Charles and Porte d'Aix Focusing on cleaning up the area around the city's main bus and train stations. Installation of open green expanses and student housing.

Belle de Mai Centred around the beloved **La Friche la Belle de Mai** (lafriche.org), a renovated former tobacco factory in the city's northeast. The sprawling edifice now includes an audiovisual centre, studios (where Marseille's ultra-popular answer to Eastenders, *Plus belle la vie*, is shot), performance spaces and artists' workshops. The **MuCEM Conservation Centre** is also located near here.

Rue de la République Sweeping from the back of the port to place de la Joliette, this grand *rue* marks the core of the **Opération Programmée d'Amélioration de l'Habitat (OPAH)**. The project has cleaned and restored the down-at-heel Haussmann buildings that line the street; shady trees are also due to be planted and contemporary street furniture installed by early 2013.

Cité de la Méditerranée Spanning 3 km of waterfront from the Vieux Port in the south to Arenc in the north. Projects (like so much else in the city, due for completion by early 2013) include the creation of **Esplanade du J4**, a pedestrian promenade outside of Fort St-Jean, which includes a panoramic elevated walkway; the C-shaped, semi-submerged **Centre Régional de la Méditerranée**, to house exhibition spaces, boutiques, cafés and private residences; the wide **Esplanade de la Major**, in front of the Cathédrale de la Major will be home to a 53-m fountain and the expanded ferry terminal; the **Euromed Center**, Italian architect Massimiliano Fuksas's futuristic new cultural complex housing a Marriott hotel, convention centre and film director Luc Besson's multiplex cinema; the redeveloped **Quais d'Arenc**, which will include international shipping group CMA CGM's 33-floor skyscraper designed by award-winning architect Zaha Hadid, Le Silo, Arenc's former silos transformed into a performance centre, and four office and apartment blocks, designed by Jean Nouvel, Yves Lion, Jean Baptiste Pietri and Roland Carta (lesquaisdarenc.fr); and the new **MuCEM**.

Fonds Régional d'Art Contemporain de Marseille (FRAC)
ⓘ *20 boulevard de Dunkerque, T04 91 91 27 55, fracpaca.org. Tue-Sat 1400-1800. Free. M2 to 'Joliette', T2. Map: Marseille, C2, p24.*
One of Marseille's finest contemporary art venues even when based in its previous, petite Le Panier premises, FRAC is due to inaugurate its brand-new cutting-edge space in early 2013. Designed by Japanese architect Kengo Kuma, FRAC's new visually arresting glass facade shelters two temporary exhibition spaces, as well as a cafe-restaurant, resident studios, a plateau expérimental for live performances and a panoramic terrace.

Musée des Civilisations de l'Europe et de la Méditerranée (MuCEM)
ⓘ *Fort St-Jean, entrance for L'Espace Georges Henri Rivière at Esplanade St-Jean, entrance for La Tour du Roy René at quai du Port, T04 96 13 80 90, mucem.org. Opening hours vary, many exhibitions free. Buses 55 and 83. Map: Marseille, B3, p24.*
Housed within the refreshed 17th-century Fort St-Jean, MuCEM organises temporary exhibitions dedicated to folk art, culture and traditions of the Mediterranean. Construction

of J4, a contemporary cube-shaped edifice that will house MuCEM's permanent collection as well as temporary shows, is nearing completion to the Fort's west. It's been designed by architects Rudy Riciotti and Roland Carta, and is due to open to the public in early 2013.

Les Docks de la Joliette
ⓘ *10 place de la Joliette. M2 to 'Joliette' and T2. Map: Marseille, B1, p24.*
Constructed over the decade between 1856 and 1866, the Joliette Docks originally served as Marseille's primary warehouse, storing the bulk cargoes that flooded into France's biggest commercial port. Reflecting the structure's historic importance, renovations of the building were the first project undertaken under the city's Euroméditerranée project (see page 27). Work was led by architect Eric Castaldi and completed in 2002. The 80,000 sq m edifice is now part of the economic fabric of Marseille and houses 250 businesses, plus several restaurants and shops.

Basilique de Notre-Dame-de-la-Garde
ⓘ *Rue Fort du Sanctuaire, T04 91 13 40 80, notredamedelagarde.com. Apr-Sep daily 0700-1915, Oct-Mar daily 0700-1815. Free. Bus 60. Map: Marseille, C6, p24.*
Also referred to as 'La Bonne Mère' ('the Good Mother'). The cathedral's 10-m gilded Madonna has been casting a protective eye over the city's fishermen since its consecration in 1864. Built on the site of a 13th-century chapel, the Romanesque-Byzantine basilica was designed by Henri Espérandieu and completed by his student, Henri Révoil; the interior is a tapestry of colours, shimmering with mosaics and golden statues. The cathedral is positioned on Marseille's highest natural point, and is visible everywhere from the Vieux Port to the Prado beaches, making for fantastic views from outside the church itself.

Cours Julien
ⓘ *M2 to Notre-Dame-du-Mont (Cours Julien), buses 41 and 81. Map: Marseille, F4, p180.*
A network of one-off boutiques, galleries, bars and terraced restaurants, the neighbourhood around pedestrianised cours Julien makes for a pleasant wander, night or day. Nearby, **Le Palais des Arts** ⓘ *1 place Carli, T04 91 42 51 50, museeregardsdeprovence.com, daily 1000-1800, €5, €2.80 16-18s, €2 students/12-15s, under 11s free*, hosts celebrated exhibitions, including the recent 'Jean Cocteau et la Méditerranée', as well as concerts.

Abbaye de St-Victor
ⓘ *3 rue de l'Abbaye, T04 96 11 22 60, saintvictor.net. Daily 0900-1900. Basilica free, crypts €2, €1 child. Map: Marseille, B5, p24.*
On the southern side of the Vieux Port, this imposing abbey was built during the 13th century to replace an original fifth-century church, destroyed by Saracen invaders 200 years earlier. Its crypts house a creepy necropolis (second century BC to the early Christian era), as well as the Abbey's famous 'Black Madonna' statue.

For over four decades, the Abbey has been hosting **Le Festival de Musique** ⓘ *T04 91 05 84 48, saintvictor.chez.com*, during October and November, although its most popular festival is its **Candlemas** celebrations (Feb).

Vallon des Auffes
ⓘ *Bus 83. Map: Marseille, A5, p24.*
Petite, pastel and a striking contrast to Marseille's often-gritty streets, Vallon des Auffes is a half-hour stroll from the Vieux Port. Equal parts fishing boats and charming cottages,

it's also a restaurant Mecca. For a treat, **Chez Fonfon** (chez-fonfon.com) and **L'Epuisette** (l-epuisette.com) are both exquisite dining options.

Back on the main corniche stands Sartorio's World War I memorial, **Monument aux Morts des Armées d'Orient**, while further south is César's propeller-like **Monument aux Repatriés d'Afrique du Nord**.

The Frioul Islands and north of Marseille

Close enough to be considered suburbs, the Frioul Islands, around 20 minutes off Marseille's coast, and L'Estaque and the Côte Bleue Calanques, just northwest of the city, are all ideal escapes when the urban jungle becomes a little too oppressive. Further north, Martigues is a charming mini-Venice, rarely visited by tourists.

Château d'If
ⓘ T04 91 59 02 30, if.monuments-nationaux.fr. Mid May-mid Sep 0940-1740, mid Sep-mid May 0930-1730, closed Mon mid Sep-mid May. €5.50, €4 18-25s, under 18s free, EU citizens under 26 free.
On the smallest island in the Frioul Archipelago and clearly visible from Marseille's shoreline, the Château d'If was built under François I in 1524. The sandy stone structure served as both a fortress and a prison, but it's perhaps best known as the fictional setting for Alexandre Dumas' *Le Comte de Monte-Cristo*.

To clamber over the Château and its island, hop aboard the **Frioul If Express** *ⓘ 1 quai des Belges, T04 96 11 03 50, frioul-if-express.com, €10 return*, a frequent ferry service that runs from the Vieux Port and on to the Frioul Islands. It's well worth hopping over to explore the two largest, Pomègues and Ratonneau, which are connected by a man-made bridge. These islands boast walking trails, turquoise inlets, harbourside restaurants and beachy coves. For more information about the Frioul and Riou Archipelagos, see ilesdemarseille.fr (French only).

L'Estaque
ⓘ Bus 35 from place de la Joliette.
Formerly a stand-alone fishing village, l'Estaque became a popular destination for artists after Paul Cézanne set up his easel here in 1870; painters Raoul Dufy, André Derain, Georges Braque and Renoir quickly shadowed his footsteps. Today, you too can make like the modern masters: the Marseille Tourist Office hands out maps of l'Estaque printed with two walking routes, the **Grand** and **Petit Chemins de Peintres**.

The Côte Bleue Calanques
Limestone cliffs, or *calanques*, surround Marseille, making both for jaw-dropping landscapes and a range of outdoor activities. To the west of l'Estaque, turquoise coves are tucked among the pines and the rugged shoreline, including the **Calanques du Jonquier** and **de l'Everine**, west of Niolon, **Calanque de Méjean** and **Calanque de la Redonne**. All are peppered with much-coveted weekend homes belonging mainly to wealthy Marseillaise. Pack a picnic lunch and take your pick. Further along are the buzzy beach resorts of **Carry-le-Rouet** and **Sausset-les-Pins**.

For information about the more frequently visited Calanques near Cassis, to the southeast of Marseille, see page 37.

Martigues

On the edge of the vast Etang de Berre, Martigues is made up of three distinct areas, all formerly villages in their own right. The **Martigues Tourist Office** ① *Rond-point de l'Hôtel-de-Ville, T04 42 42 31 10, martigues-tourisme.com*, is located near the Hôtel de Ville, west along the northern shore in Ferrières. Pleasantly unpretentious, the latter's open squares are lined with yellow and pink buildings. Nearby, the **Musée Ziem** ① *bd du 14 Juillet, T04 42 41 39 60, Jul-Aug 1000-1200 and 1430-1830, Sep-Jun Wed-Mon 1430-1830, free*, celebrates turn-of-the-century artist Félix Ziem, who painted landscapes of the local spot known as *Miroir aux Oiseaux*. The museum also includes pieces by other great artists of the period, such as Paul Signac and François Picabia. To the south, a residential island laced with waterways sits in the middle of the Canal de Caronte, while across another bridge is the more affluent Jonquières neighbourhood.

Marseille and around listings

For hotel and restaurant price codes and other relevant information, see pages 10-14.

🛏 Where to stay

Marseille *p23, map p24*

€€€€ Le Petit Nice Passédat, *Anse de Maldormé, corniche JF Kennedy, T04 91 59 25 92, passedat.fr*. Managed by three generations of the Passédat family since it opened in 1917, this petite enclave of exclusivity draws luxury-seekers and a celebrity clientele. Rooms are sea-facing, and there's a stunning garden terrace and heated outdoor pool, plus renowned gastronomic restaurant. Worth the splurge.

€€€€-€€€ Villa Massalia, *17 place Louis Bonnefon, T04 91 72 90 00, concorde-hotels. com*. In a smart residential district near the Stade Vélodrome and a favourite with visiting footballers, Villa Massalia is modern luxury all the way: Nespresso machine in each spacious room, hammam, fitness area, sauna and outdoor pool (non-guests welcome, €45). Local fishermen provide daily fresh fish for the Yin Yang Chinese restaurant, on site.

€€€ New Hôtel Vieux Port, *3bis rue Reine Elisabeth, T04 91 99 23 23, new-hotel.com*. Spacious, subtly themed rooms (African, Land of the Rising Sun, Arabian Nights) steps from the port and La Canebière.

Flat-screen TVs, and some rooms boast private balconies. Discount packages, particularly on weekends.

€€€-€€ Aux Vieux Panier, *13 rue du Panier, T04 91 91 23 72, auvieuxpanier.com*. A hip new addition to Marseille's sleeping scene. Nestled into the heart of Le Panier, this petite bed and breakfast boasts just five contemporary rooms, each one designed by a different international artist. Panoramic rooftop terrace to boot.

€€€-€€ Hôtel du Palais, *26 rue Breteuil, T04 91 37 78 86, hoteldupalaismarseille. com*. A few blocks south of the Vieux Port in a semi-residential neighbourhood, this affable spot makes a good base for sightseeing. Rooms are small but modern, staff are welcoming and there's free Wi-Fi. Recommended.

€€€-€€ Hôtel Hermes, *12 rue Bonneterie, T04 96 11 63 63, hotelmarseille. com*. Twenty-nine basic rooms, some with views over the port, at the foot of the Panier district. There's a fantastic roof terrace, and kitsch but appealing murals of ancient Greece adorning the breakfast room walls downstairs.

€€€-€€ Hôtel Le Corbusier, *280 bd Michelet, T04 91 16 78 00, hotellecorbusier. com*. A site of architectural pilgrimage, also referred to as 'Unité d'Habitation' and 'la Cité Radieuse'. Designed by Swiss architect

Le Corbusier and constructed during the late 1940s, this structure was originally intended to help stem the period's drastic housing shortage. The hotel's cabin rooms and studios are spread over two of the building's floors.

€€€-€€ Hôtel St Ferréol, *19 rue Pisançon (corner rue St Ferréol), T04 91 33 12 21, hotel-stferreol.com.* Friendly bargain spot in the heart of Marseille's shopping district. The 19 rooms – some standard, some superior – are small but neat, and have a/c and free Wi-Fi. Bargain rates available out of season.

€€ Hôtel Péron, *119 corniche JF Kennedy, T04 91 31 01 41, hotel-peron.com.* Friendly, family-run spot between downtown Marseille and Vallon des Auffes. Funky, 1960s decor dotted throughout; best are the corner rooms, which look out over Château d'If and the Frioul islands.

🍴 Restaurants

Marseille *p23, map p24*

Plenty of restaurants include Marseille's most famous dish on their menus. But how do you know if the fish stew on offer is the genuine stuff? Traditional *bouillabaisse* should include at least four different fish (take your pick of red mullet, John Dory, conger eel, skate or scorpion fish); monkfish and spiny lobster are optional. The fish should be cooked in a tomato and rockfish stock, along with potatoes. *Bouillabaisse* is eaten as two courses – first the soup, then the fish, which must be deboned and prepared in front of the diner. *Rouille*, a saffron and paprika mayonnaise, is served alongside. If you want to be really sure you're dining on *la vraie bouillabaisse*, check if the restaurant is a member of **La Charte de la Bouillabaisse Marseillaise**. This local stamp of approval guarantees authenticity; of the mere eleven restaurants the charter recognises, seven are in Marseille. And finally, remember other restaurants do dish up excellent renditions of *bouillabaisse*, even if they bend the authentic guidelines laid out here.

€€€€ Chez Michel, *6 rue des Catalans, T04 91 52 30 63, restaurant-michel-13.fr. Daily 1200-1400 and 2000-2200.* Across from the pretty Plage des Catalans and with views out to Château d'If, this spot is recommended by locals time and again for their choice *bouillabaisse* (€60 per person); the *bourride* (a fish stew variation, blended with garlicky aïoli, €53 per person) is also delectable. Under family management since 1946.

€€€€ Restaurant Le Rhul, *corniche J F Kennedy, T04 91 52 54 54, lerhul.fr. Daily 1200-1400 and 1900-2200.* One of the city's finest spots to dine on traditional *bouillabaisse*; the menu also features a range of excellent fish and seafood dishes. As favoured by Jacques Chirac and French celebrities.

€€€-€€ Toinou, *3 cours St-Louis, T0811 45 45 45, toinou.com. Daily 1100-2300.* Oysters, urchins, crab and plenty more at this relaxed seafood specialist, a Marseillaise favourite for over four decades. Self-catering? Pick up your own spread from the restaurant's kiosk outside.

€€ Bar de la Marine, *15 quai de Rive Neuve, T04 91 54 95 42. Daily 0700-0200.* The easygoing port-side bar featured in Marcel Pagnol's novels and films, *Marius, Fanny*, and *César*; it was also a Portuguese stand-in for a scene in the film *Love Actually*. Good salads ('La Marine' features red mullet, sardines and salmon, €11) and *steak haché* (€14).

€€ Le Grain du Sel, *39 rue de la Paix Marcel Paul, T04 91 54 47 30. Tue-Sat 1230-1330 and 2000-2130.* Although it only opened its doors in 2011, Le Grain du Sel is already a firm favourite on the Marseillaise dining scene. Produce is farm-fresh – Chef Pierre Giannetti sources many of his seasonal ingredients from his farm in nearby

Martigues – and lunchtime menus (€14-17) are a steal. Reservations recommended.

€ Pizzeria Etienne, *43 rue de Lorette*, T04 91 54 76 33. *Mon-Sat 1230-1400 and 1800-2300*. Tucked away in Le Panier's back streets, Etienne's decor is pleasantly dated and the delectable menu brief: half-anchovy, half-cheese pizza (for one-four diners), *côte de bœuf* (rib steak, for one-three diners) and a smattering of starters. Well worth seeking out.

Cafés and bars

Green Bear Coffee, *17 rue Glandevès*, T04 91 04 06 91, greenbearcoffee.com. *Mon-Sat 0930-1530*. All-organic, tiny coffee bar and lunchtime café tucked behind the Vieux Port. Daily offerings include a *plat du jour*, such as *gratin des légumes* (€6.80), a choice of tarts (look out for the tasty mushroom and smoked tofu quiche, €4.80) and a homemade soup (recently a creamy celery and chestnut, €4.20).

OM Café, *25 quai des Belges*, T04 91 33 80 33. *Daily 0900-2300*. Join supporters of local football team Olympique Marseille (OM) for this spot's tasty bistro fare: *entrecôte*, or *marmite du pêcheur*. There are plenty of big screens dotted around on match nights.

Oscar's, *8 quai Rive Neuve*, T04 91 33 28 86. *Daily 1000-2100*. The Vieux Port's favourite New York-style locale, serving up bagels, doughnuts and big cups of coffee. Best is the Classic Bagel Sandwich (€5.70), stuffed with smoked salmon, cream cheese, red onions and capers.

Pâtisserie d'Aix, *2 rue d'Aix*, T04 91 90 12 50. *Tue-Sun 0900-1800*. Cosy North African pastry shop near the city's Bibliothèque de l'Alcazar, serving glasses of tasty mint tea among their heavenly pyramids of sticky sweets.

Niolon

€€€-€€ Auberge du Mérou, *Calanque de Niolon*, T04 91 46 98 69, aubergedumerou. fr. *Daily 1200-1400, Tue-Sat 1930-2130*.

Dine on seafood, just metres above the turquoise sea. Best is their ultra-fresh fish, simply grilled or cooked in a salt crust. The Auberge also has five basic bedrooms (€), half-board optional.

Martigues *p31*

€€€-€€ Le Bouchon à la Mer, *19 quai Lucien Toulmond*, T04 42 49 41 41, lebouchonalamer.eresto.net. *Tue-Sun 1230-1400 and 1900-2200*. Contemporary French cuisine, from local chef Christophe Perrin. Go for the rabbit terrine, served with a coriander salad, or treat yourself to the decadent foie gras and poached oysters in truffle sauce.

🎭 Entertainment

Marseille *p23, map p24*
In Marseille, get the lowdown on what's going down (club nights, new shops, current exhibitions) with one of these free newspapers: **L'Hebdo** (French, marseillelhebdo.com); **COTE** (French/English, cotemagazine.com); **Ventilo** (French, journalventilo.fr); **César** (French).

Clubs and bars

La Caravelle, *34 quai du Port*, T04 91 90 36 64, lacaravelle-marseille.fr. *Daily 0700-0100*. Aperitifs from 1800 with amazing tapas, overlooking the Vieux Port. Live music Wednesday and Friday evenings.

Le Cri du Port, *8 rue du Pasteur Heuzé*, T04 91 50 51 41, criduport.fr. International jazz acts, most evenings (Thu-Sun 2030).

The New Cancan, *3-7 rue Sénac*, T04 91 48 59 76, newcancan.com. *Thu-Sun 2300-dawn*. The city's best gay club pulls in a mixed crowd.

Le Pelle-Mêle, *8 place aux Huiles*, T04 91 54 85 26. *Mon-Sat 1800-0200*, live shows usually Fri and Sat 2230. Local and international jazz concerts from €4; also a great place for a late night drink.

Le Polikarpov, *24 cours Honoré d'Estienne d'Orves, T04 91 52 70 30, lepolikarpov.com. Daily 0900-0200.* Tiny vodka bar, with temporary art installations and live DJs most weekends.

Trolleybus, *24 quai Rive Neuve, T04 91 54 30 45, letrolley.com. Wed-Sat, from 2300.* Enduringly popular port-side club since its opening in 1989, playing 80s, house and disco. For both club nights and theatre performances, see also **La Friche la Belle de Mai** (page 28).

Sports

Stade Vélodrome, *3 bd Michelet, om.net.* Sixty-thousand-seat Olympique de Marseille stadium; football matches and other sporting events.

Theatre

Opéra Municipal de Marseille,
2 rue Molière, T04 91 55 11 10, opera. marseille.fr. Opera and ballet performances from September-June.

Théâtre National de la Criée, *30 quai Rive Neuve, T04 91 54 70 54, theatre-lacriee.com. Closed Aug.* Premier theatre, located within the city's former fish market.

⊙ Shopping

Marseille *p23, map p24*
Art and antiques
d+ design, *52 rue de Lorette, T06 89 13 49 77. Tue-Sat 1100-1900.* Lamps, furnishings and kitchenware from the 1950s-70s.

Books
Librairie-Galerie Imbernon, *280 bd Michelet, Le Corbusier no357, T04 91 22 56 84, editionsimbernon.com. Tue-Sat 0930-1300 and 1500-1930.* Architecture book specialist.

Clothes and shoes
Antoine & Lili, *38 rue Montgrand, T04 91 52 73 70, antoineetlili.com. Mon, Wed-Thu 1030-1330 and 1430-1930, Tue and Fri-Sat*

1000-2000. Paris-based brand, selling dashing Asian-inspired clothes and shoes for women.

La Compagnie de Provence Marseille,
18 rue Francis Davso, T04 91 33 04 17, compagniedeprovence.com. Mon-Sat 1000-1900. Natural soaps and creams, locally produced.

Esprit-Raphia, *15 cours Julien, T04 91 94 03 86, esprit-raphia.com.* Handmade leather and canvas espadrilles: pick up a pair (each one is unique) or ask Annie to make the shoes of your dreams.

La Sardine à Paillettes, *9 rue de la Tour, T04 91 91 63 28, lasardineapaillettes. com. Mon 1400-1900, Tue-Sat 1030-1330 and 1430-1900.* Fabulous kids' clothes from Danish designer Louise Hjorth, plus Japanese lunchboxes, tights and bags.

Repetto, *24 rue Francis Davso, T04 91 91 53 09, repetto.fr. Mon-Sat 1000-1900.* Soft leather ballerina shoes, created for French dancers, now internationally coveted.

Food and drink
Four des Navettes, *136 rue Sainte, T04 91 33 32 12, fourdesnavettes.com. Sep-Jul Mon-Sat 0700-2000, Sun and Aug 0900-1300 and 1500-1930.* Marseille's oldest bakery (founded in 1781) and purveyors of *navettes*, the city's famous orange-blossom, cakey biscuits. From €8.50 per dozen.

Maison de Pastis, *108 quai du Port, T04 91 90 86 77. Mon-Fri 1030-1900, Sat 1000-1900, Sun 1030-1700.* For all things pastis: pick up big brands or herby artisan specials.

Markets
All of the following markets run from 0800-1300, except where indicated. For the biggest bargains, it's best to arrive very early or very late.

Vieux Port Fish Market, *Quai des Belges (daily)* and **Flower Market** *(Tue and Sat)*. One of the few city markets where fishermen still pitch up to ply their own catch.

Marché des Capucins, *Place des Capucins.*
Mon-Sat 0800-1900. Cheap wholesale fruit
and veg, plus North African nibbles.
Cours Julien Organic Market, *Wed.*
Sheep's cheese, an organic butcher,
honey and wine; look out for Sisteron-
based bakery La Paline's famous *fougasse
à l'anchois.*
Marché aux Puces, *Chemin de la Madrague
Ville. Sun 0600-1300.* Massive flea market
north of the city centre.

⚙ What to do

Marseille *p23, map p24*
Cultural
Idées Seniors, *idees-seniors.com, available
at the Marseille Tourist Office.* Seasonal
magazine listing quality activities and
excursions aimed at the city's older visitors.
Families with little ones can look out for
the magazine *Idées Enfants* (ideesdenfants.
com) instead, by the same publisher. Both
in French.

Food and wine
Bouillabaisse Cooking Lesson, *T04
91 13 89 00, marseille-tourisme.com.*
Once a month, the Marseille Tourist
Office organises a *bouillabaisse* lesson in
collaboration with Restaurant Miramar.
€120 per person.

⊖ Transport

Marseille *p23, map p24*
Marseille is a hilly town, although the
energetic will have no problem navigating
the downtown area on foot. Marseille has
two tram lines. The most useful for tourists
is T2, which runs along La Canebière and
northwards to place de la Joliette. There
are two metro lines, linking Gare St-Charles
with the Vieux Port (M1) or place Castellane,
the Stade Vélodrome and points south
(M2). The city is also home to an extensive
network of buses, which will get you

anywhere else you need to go. The same
ticket is valid for travel on buses, trams or
on the metro; a single ride on any of these
costs €1.50. If you plan to use a fair amount
of public transport, or are in town for a
few days, it's worth buying a *carte journée*
(day pass, €5) or carnet of tickets (10 rides
€12.60). You can buy tickets in metro
stations, on the bus or from automatic
kiosks at each tram stop. Note that tickets
are not sold on trams, and you must
validate your ticket at one of the small,
freestanding machines before boarding. For
further information about public transport
in Marseille, see rtm.fr. Taxi stands are
dotted around town, including one in the
northeast corner of the Vieux Port (across
from Bar de la Samaritaine); you can also
arrange a pick-up by contacting **Taxi Radio
Marseille** (T04 91 02 20 20 , taximarseille.
com). Although plenty of ferries run trips
to the nearby Calanques, they're always
return excursions, rather than an actual
means of transport.

Marseille Provence Airport
(mrsairport.com) is around 25 km
west of the city centre. Shuttle buses
(navettemarseilleaeroport.com) run
between the airport and Marseille's bus
station at Gare St-Charles, rue Honnorat
every 15-20 minutes (25 mins); there
are also shuttles to Aix-en-Provence
(navetteaixtgvaeroport.com, 30 mins,
departures every half hour).

Various companies run **ferries** from
Marseille to Corsica, Sardinia, Tunisia and
Algeria. See the following websites for
prices and schedules: SNCM (sncm.fr),
Compagnie Tunisienne de Navigation (ctn.
com.tn) and Algérie Ferries (algerieferries.
com). Ferry station: Place de la Joliette
and boulevard des Dames.

There are frequent trains from Marseille
to Cassis (25 mins), La Ciotat (35 mins),
Bandol (45 mins), Sanary-sur-Mer (50 mins)
and Toulon (40 mins-1 hr). Trains every
one to two hours along the Côte Bleue to

Martigues (45 mins). The train station is on Gare St-Charles, square Narvik.

Martigues *p31*

Trains every one to two hours along the Côte Bleue to Marseille (45 mins).

❶ Directory

Marseille *p23, map p24*
Money ATMs throughout the city. **Medical services** Hôpital de la Timone, 264 rue St-Pierre, T04 91 49 91 91, ap-hm.fr.

Pharmacie Tran Nghi, 10 cours Belsunce, T04 91 90 14 58. **Post office** 1 cours Jean Ballard. **Tourist information office** 4 la Canebière (Vieux Port), T0826 500 500, marseille-tourisme.com, (Mon-Sat 0900-1900, Sun and holidays 1000-1700). If you plan to buckle down for some heavy sightseeing, pick up a City Pass (one day €22, two days €29) from the Tourist Office. The Pass gives the holder free entrance to 14 museums and monuments, return boat trips to Château d'If and all public transport for its duration.

Cassis and the Calanques

Southeast of Marseille, the Massif des Calanques comprises close to 20 km of rocky limestone cliffs, deep inlets and translucent waters. Trails tangle through the wilderness, making the 4000-ha protected area best explored on foot or by boat.

It was here in 1985 that local boy Henri Cosquer discovered a stunning Ice Age cave, its walls decorated with hundreds of animal paintings (approximately 18,000 years old) and hand tracings, dating from around 27,000 years ago. Inaccessible to the public after three divers died trying to reach the cave in 1992, the entrance to the Grotte Cosquer lies at 37 m below sea level, between the Calanques of Sormiou and Morgiou.

Sandwiched between the Massif des Calanques and Cap Canaille, the latter boasting Europe's second highest sea cliff (Grand Tête, 394 m), the fishing village of Cassis has always been one of the southern French coast's most enchanting. Paul Signac painted the bay and headlands in 1899; Winston Churchill took art lessons here in 1920, bedding down at the Hotel Panorama (now the Camargo Foundation cultural centre, camargofoundation.org); and Virginia Woolf and friends spent long periods in Cassis during the 1930s, staying with her sister, Vanessa Bell.

Cassis, although certainly a lot busier, retains its appeal today. A medieval castle overlooks the town's harbour, which in turn is packed with traditional wooden fishing boats and pleasure craft. Kiosks selling sea urchins line the quays, opposite terraced restaurants and pavement cafés. North of town there are inland valleys of vineyards, renowned for their production of crisp white wine. Just a small percentage of this hand-harvested nectar is exported abroad, making the AOC area (just 196 ha) still the best place to sample it.

Visiting the Calanques by boat

GIE des Bateliers Cassidains

ⓘ *Cassis port, cassis-calanques.com; a full list of boats and contact telephone numbers can be downloaded from the website. Tours: three Calanques (Port Miou, Port Pin and En Vau): Feb-Oct daily 0930-1700 every half hour, Nov-Feb from 1030 by reservation only, 45-min boat ride. €15, €9 under 10s. Five Calanques (as above, plus L'Oule and Devenson): Feb-Oct daily 1130, 1200, 1500, 1530, 1630, 1700, 65-min boat ride. €18, €12 under 10s. Eight Calanques (as above, plus L'Oeil de Verre, Sugiton and Morgiou): Feb-Oct daily 1030, 1100, 1330, 1400, 1430, 1600, 90-min boat ride. €21, €15 under 10s. Tickets on sale at the port's yellow kiosk 30 mins before departures.* During the summer months, setting out to see the Calanques from the water can be one of the region's most relaxing activities. As these organised tours chug westwards, it's increasingly difficult to believe you're less than half an hour from Marseille's urban mass.

Note that you're rarely allowed to hop off the Calanques tour boats before they arrive back in Cassis. However, occasional summer morning tours will allow you to descend at En Vau: inquire at the yellow boat kiosk in Cassis's port. From here you can swim, snorkel and then hike back to town (see below).

If you'd rather captain your own ship, **JCF Boat Services** ⓘ *jcf-boat-services.com*, rents large and small motorboats (half days from €100, excluding petrol). For a more physical experience, paddle around the inlets in one of **Cassis Sports Loisirs Nautiques**' one- or two-person kayaks; prices start at €25 per half day, see cassis-kayak.fr.

Visiting the Calanques from Marseille

To access the Massif from Marseille, take bus no 21 from La Canebière to Luminy. From here you can hike into the Calanques. Bus 23 departs from Rond-Point du Prado; its two destinations allow access to the Calanques Sormiou and Morgiou respectively. Marseille's Tourist Office also organises group walks through expert local guide **Jean Marc Nardini** ⓘ *T06 77 07 83 36, €25 per person, walks last around 3 hrs and are suitable for all fitness levels, as well as kids age 6 and above.* Alternatively, **Bleu Evasion** ⓘ *bleu-evasion.com*, runs boat tours from Marseille's Vieux Port or the more southerly Port de la Pointe Rouge.

Exploring Cassis and the Calanques on foot

All of Cassis's town maps are marked with a variety of hiking trails. Easiest is the two-hour **Vin et Terroir** walk, looping past all twelve of the town's vineyards, plus olive groves and traditional stone *bastides*.

For limestone cliffs, turquoise waters and isolated beaches, head west out of town, through residential neighbourhoods, following **La Presqu'île** to Calanque de Port-Miou (45 minutes). Keep on along the **Entre Terre et Mer** (Between Land and Sea, one hour) trail; the more ambitious can continue hiking **Les Calanques** (four-six hours), a difficult path that explores the Calanques de Port Pin and d'En Vau, plus the valley behind the two. Kids will enjoy **Le Sentier du Petit Prince** (1½ hours): leave your wheels at the Presqu'île car park, then head off to explore Cap Cable.

Cap Canaille and the **Route des Crêtes**, covering the 12 km between Cassis and La Ciotat, offer some of the coast's most breathtaking panoramas. The two long circuits over this headland involve lengthy, steep climbs: be sure you're prepared in terms of appropriate footwear, drinking water and level of physical fitness.

Five of the best Calanques

Sormiou The largest, sheltered by cliffs to the east and west. The wide sandy beach is easily accessed, and there's a restaurant open from April-September and car park.

Morgiou Crowded with fishing boats and home to one restaurant. Follow the trail skirting the shore eastwards for isolated beaches, and on to the hard-to-reach Calanque de Sugiton.

Devenson Rugged, windy cliffs and sheer sea drops that will appeal to hardcore rock-climbers. Arrive on foot, or park up at the La Gardiole car park (closed Jun-Sep).

En Vau Possibly the prettiest. Access is steep and difficult (unless you arrive by boat) but the clear waters, white sand and shingle beach are well worth the effort. No nearby spots to pick up snacks, so pack a picnic lunch.

Port Pin The smallest, with a petite beach ringed by Aleppo pines. Moderately difficult access via 'Les 3 Calanques' trail from Cassis.

Cassis and the Calanques listings

For hotel and restaurant price codes and other relevant information, see pages 10-14.

pitches for tents, trailers and campervans. No reservations accepted.

🛏 Where to stay

Cassis *p37*
See also Restaurants, below, for additional accommodation options in Cassis.
€€€€ Maison°9, *Quartier Les Janots, 9 av du Docteur Yves Bourde, T04 42 08 35 86, maison9.net. Closed Nov-Mar.* Luxury B&B set just out of town among Cassis's vineyards. The three suites have private terraces and mini-kitchenettes. Breakfasts feature home-made and locally sourced ingredients. There's also an outdoor pool, fruit garden and *pétanque* area.
€€€ Hôtel de la Plage Mahogany, *19 av de l'Amiral Ganteaume, T04 42 01 05 70, hotelmahogany.com.* A beach-lover's dream, just over the road from the Plage de Bestouan. The 30 rooms are a mix of bright colours and modern decor (sea-facing) and subdued Provençal hues (overlooking the garden). A short walk into town. Rates include breakfast.

Camping
Camping les Cigales, *Av Marne, T04 42 01 07 34, campingcassis.com. Mid Mar-mid Nov, €6.65 per person, €2.60 under 7s, €5 per pitch.* Pleasant campsite 1.5 km out of Cassis, with

🍴 Restaurants

Cassis *p37*
€€€ Le Clos des Arômes, *10 rue Abbé Paul Mouton, T04 42 01 71 84, le-clos-des-aromes. com. Tue-Sun 1200-1500 and 1930-2300, closed Jan-Feb.* Provençal dining within a lovely walled garden, under the canopy of a giant fig tree. Set menus (€26-€41) feature *daube* ravioli, *moules farcis gratinées* and veggie lasagne. Fourteen simple double rooms (€€) also on site.
€€€ Fleurs de Thym, *5 rue La Martime, T04 42 01 23 03, fleursdethym.com. Daily 1930-2300, closed Nov-Jan.* Creative Mediterranean cooking. Unusual dishes include a trio of filet mignon (beef, veal and pork), or an asparagus, smoked duck, Parmesan and vanilla-infused olive oil salad. During warmer months, white wooden tables spill on to the quiet road out front. Menus from €29.
€€€ Restaurant Nino, *1 quai Jean-Jacques Barthélemy, T04 42 01 74 32, nino-cassis. com. Tue-Sun 1200-1530, Tue-Sat 1800-2330.* Elegant yet unpretentious. Garlic wafts from the open kitchen; choose between the three-course set menu (€34) or specialities like *rascasse au basilic* (basil-drenched

scorpion fish). Nino also offers stylish accommodation (one double, two duplex suites, breakfast included €€€) overlooking Cassis's port.

€€€-€€ Poissonnerie Laurent, *6 quai Jean-Jacques Barthélemy, T04 42 01 71 56. Tue-Sun 1200-1330, Jun-Sep Tue-Sat 1930-2200, closed Jan.* Half fish shop, half restaurant, port-side Poissonnerie Laurent has been running under the same family management since 1880. Dishes of the day include *petit bourride* (€16), and the menu is littered with fabulous fish *tartares*, scallops and rockfish included. No credit cards.

€€ La Bonaparte, *14 rue du Général Bonaparte, T04 42 01 80 84. Tue-Sun 1200-1400 and 1930-2230.* Friendly budget spot on Cassis's back streets, owned by the gregarious Jean-Marie. Go for the very good *soupe de poissons* or daily fish specials; be sure to book in advance, particularly on summer evenings.

O Shopping

Cassis *p37*

L'Eau de Cassis, *2 place Barganon, T04 42 01 25 21, leaudecassis.com. Mon-Sat 1000-1300 and 1500-1900.* Creating natural perfumes since 1851.

⊖ Transport

Cassis *p37*
Cassis is tiny, and its village roads and pedestrian port are best explored on foot. Buses run to and from the train station, which is at Place de la Gare, 3.5 km outside of the town centre. There's a taxi stand (T04 42 01 78 96) next to the yellow boat kiosk in Cassis's harbour. A car can be useful for getting around the coastal region, particularly out of season; car parks are placed around town and are well signposted.

Frequent trains west to Marseille (25 mins); east to La Ciotat (10 mins), Bandol (20 mins), Sanary-sur-Mer (25 mins) and Toulon (35 mins). Four to five daily buses to La Ciotat (15 mins).

❶ Directory

Cassis *p37*
Note that most shops and services are all concentrated in Cassis: make sure you've stocked up on food, drink and any essentials before exploring the surrounding Calanques. **Medical services Pharmacie Trossero**, 11 avenue Victor Hugo, T04 42 01 70 03. **Money** Various ATMs in Cassis, including one on quai Jean-Jacques Barthélemy. **Post office** Rue de l'Arène, T04 42 01 98 30. **Tourist information Quai des Moulins**, T08 92 25 98 92, ot-cassis. fr (Jul-Aug Mon-Sat 0900-1900, Sun 0930-1230 and 1500-1800, May-Jun and Sep Mon-Sat 0900-1800, Sun 0930-1230 and 0900-1830, Mar-Apr and Oct Mon-Sat 0930-1230 and 1430-1800, Sun 1000-1230, Nov-Feb Mon-Sat 0930-1230 and 1400-1700, Sun 1000-1230).

Bandol and around

The seaside resort of Bandol is this area's most famous, drawing visitors with its unaffected attitude and luscious wines. But the surrounding hilltop villages and coastal towns – plus the offshore islands of Ile de Bendor, Ile Verte and Ile des Embiez – each hold their own unique appeal.

Bandol → *For listings, see pages 43-46.*

Mention 'Bandol' to any French person, and the first association is likely to be one of the south of France's finest appellations. While the Bandol region is known to produce a tasty vintage, the town itself is a popular coastal resort: more sand castles, chips and kids than elegant old quaffers.

But it wasn't always so. During the late 19th and early 20th centuries, Bandol provided creative inspiration to German writer Thomas Mann, who stayed at the beachfront Grand Hôtel, and New Zealand-born author Katherine Mansfield. French celebrities flocked to the town, from popular cabaret performer Mistinguett to singer Henri Salvador, and Bandol's renown slowly grew.

Nowadays, a pretty, palm-lined promenade separates the compact town centre from the deep marina, while looping around past the remains of a château, **Plage de Rènecros**, is a perfect crescent of a beach. An easy, yellow-marked *sentier littoral* continues 12 km westward along the seafront from Rènecros to Les Lecques, passing **Plage de Barry** where Jacques-Yves Cousteau, Philippe Tailliez and Frédéric Dumas are said to have invented the first aqua-lung in 1943. On the other side of town, beach after beach creates a smooth succession of sun, sea and sand from the Casino most of the way to Sanary-sur-Mer.

Ile de Bendor
ⓘ *1.5 km off Bandol's coast, bendor.com. Daily ferries: Jul-Aug 0700-0215 (every 30 mins-1 hr), Apr-Jun and Sep 0700-1900 (every 30 mins-1 hr) and 1920-2400 (by advance reservation), Oct-Mar 0745-1700 (hourly); 7-min crossing. Apr-Sep €11, €9 child (2-12), under 2s free; Oct-Mar €9, €7 child (2-12), under 2s free.*
A tiny, 7-ha island just off Bandol's coast, the Ile de Bendor was purchased during the 1950s by Paul Ricard, founder of Ricard pastis. It was here that Ricard created his own unconventional world, hosting rollicking parties and entertaining the era's most sought-after socialites and celebrities, including Salvador Dali. As an amateur artist, Ricard eventually opted to transform the island into a public *île des arts*; local artisans opened ateliers, hotels and restaurants set up camp, and holidaymakers were welcomed to the island.

Today, visitors can hop on one of the frequent seven-minute ferries from Bandol's port and spend an afternoon exploring Bendor. An easy, 20-minute footpath rings the island, taking in one small sandy beach, various bathing terraces and, especially on its south side, plenty of russet rocky outcrops. The island is home to six bars and restaurants, three hotels, a helipad and the quirky **Exposition Universelle des Vins et Spiritueux** ⓘ *T04 94 05 15 61, euvs.org, Jul-Aug Thu-Tue 1300-1800, free).* Set up by Ricard in 1958, this museum is frescoed with ceiling scenes of joyful alcoholic consumption; beneath is a neat collection of more than 8000 bottles of wines and spirits, as well as old wine lists, cocktail-making instruments and other drinking paraphernalia.

During July and August, ferries also run from Sanary-sur-Mer to the island, departing from Général de Gaulle wharf (15-20 minute crossing). Note that most shops and all but two of the restaurants shut down from October to March.

Around Bandol

Le Castellet

It's mostly French visitors who flock to this medieval perched village. Built during the 12th century, control of the town bounced from the lords of Les Baux to Angevin rule (15th century), and eventually on to the Lombards, who ruled the walled stronghold until the French Revolution.

More recently, Le Castellet is most famous as the setting for Marcel Pagnol's 1938 film, *La Femme du Boulanger*. Wander within Le Castellet's ramparts, shop for unique artisan-made gifts at the town's many gallery-shops or head to *Le trou de Madame* (signposted), a balcony-like opening in the city walls, affording views all the way to the sea.

Nearby, the **Circuit Paul Ricard** (circuitpaulricard.com) hosted Formula 1 races through the 1970s and 80s, although its current competitions are more low-key.

La Cadière d'Azur

A peaceful hilltop town, La Cadière remains elegantly laid-back, even during summer's peak. Visit for the picturesque pavement cafés, shady cobbled streets and panoramic vineyard views.

St-Cyr-sur-Mer and Les Lecques

Directly west of La Cadière d'Azur and Le Castellet, Les Lecques has a magnetic appeal for families, both due to its long, sandy beach and nearby **Aqualand** ① *T04 94 32 08 32, aqualand.fr, Jul-Aug 1000-1900, mid-late Jun and 1st week Sep 1000-1800, €25, €18.50 child (3-12)/over 65, under 1 m free*.

Inland, St-Cyr's main claim to fame is its small, gold leaf-covered version of sculptor Frédéric Auguste Bartholdi's **Statue of Liberty**, which sits in place Portalis; wealthy resident Anatole Ducros donated it to the town in 1913.

La Ciotat

The bay curves westwards, Les Lecques' beach eventually merging with a strip of seafront hotels on the edge of La Ciotat. A working town, long associated with its now-defunct dockyards, La Ciotat had a brief encounter with international fame when it featured in brothers Auguste and Louis Lumière's 1898 film, *L'arrivée d'un train en gare de La Ciotat*, although viewers of the silent movie leapt out of the silent movie theatre to avoid the 'oncoming train'. The small **Espace Lumière** ① *20 rue Maréchal Foch, T04 42 08 69 60, Jul-Sep Tue and Sat 1000-1900, Wed and Fri 1500-1800, Oct-Jun Tue-Wed and Fri-Sat 1500-1800, free*, has photos and posters that document the era. And after years of renovations, the city's **Eden Cinema**, which claims to be the oldest in the world, will reopen to the public in May of 2013.

La Ciotat is home to two alluring spots of natural beauty: the **Anse de Figuerolles** and the **Ile Verte**. The former is a cool, pebbly Calanque to the west of the town, while the latter is a small island, less than 500 m by 250 m, located just off La Ciotat's coast. Frequent ferries run visitors to the island from April to September, including a special early-bird run for fishermen, departing at 0700 on weekends ① *laciotat-ileverte.com, €10 return, €6 under 10s return.*

Sanary-sur-Mer

A rosy-hued fishing village to Bandol's east, Sanary served as a safe harbour for German Jews during World War II: Bertolt Brecht and Thomas Mann both settled here, joining Aldous Huxley, also a short-term resident of the town.

Today, Sanary is a relaxed spot to be based. Its cute harbour is lined with fish restaurants, and there's a lively market here on Wednesday mornings. In the hills above the town, the child-friendly **exotic zoo** ① *Le Jardin Exotique, T04 94 29 40 38, zoosanary.com, May-Sep daily 0930-1900, Feb-Apr and Oct daily 0930-1800, Nov-Jan Wed, Sat and Sun 0930-1800, €8.50, €6 child (3-10), under 3s free,* is packed with parrots, peacocks, monkeys and a botanical garden.

South of here at Le Brusc, ferries zip along the 12-minute route to **Ile des Embiez** (lesembiez.com), another island snapped up by Paul Ricard during the 1950s. The island is home to three hotels, eight restaurants, various beaches, an Oceanographic Institute (institut-paul-ricard.org) and Domaine des Embiez, its own 10-ha vineyard. During July and August, ferries also run to and from Sanary-sur-Mer directly.

Driving the Bandol Vineyards

Close to 60 vineyards ripple through the countryside north of Bandol, producing red and rosé wines based on a majority percentage of Mourvèdre grapes. If your days sunning on the beach have begun to lose their lustre, a drive around these hilltop towns, valleys and vineyards may make for the perfect antidote.

Leave Bandol along the D559b. This northbound route heads in the direction of Le Beausset, crossing the A50 motorway along the way. To your west are the perched **Château de Pibarnon** ① *T04 94 90 12 73, pibarnon.com,* vineyards. Or opt to head east, following the signs for **Château Ste-Anne** ① *T04 94 90 35 40.* Both are family-run and welcoming, although it's best to call ahead for a (free) tour, particularly out of season. If you'd rather just cruise around, taking in the scenery, stop by **La Cadierenne** ① *off the A50 at junction 11, Quartier Le Vallon, La Cadière d'Azur, T04 94 90 11 06, cadierenne.net, Mon-Sat 0900-1200 and 1400-1730),* a cooperative selling a variety of nearby producers.

Don't have your own wheels? Time a visit to Bandol to coincide with the annual **Fête du Millésime**. Local wine producers line the port on the first Sunday in December, offering lip-smacking samples of their latest vintage.

For more information about Bandol wine and its vineyards, see vinsdebandol.com.

Bandol and around listings

For hotel and restaurant price codes and other relevant information, see pages 10-14.

⊖ Where to stay

Bandol and Ile de Bendor *p41*
€€€€-€€€ Le Delos, *Ile de Bendor, T04 94 05 90 90, bendor.com.* Designed by Paul

Ricard at the island's eastern end, Le Delos has 19 bright, unique rooms, an outdoor pool and on-site restaurant, the latter overseen by chefs Nicolas Rutard and Antonny Dubois. The hotel also manages the 36-room **Le Palais**, Ricard's take on a Venetian Palace, and eight one- and two-bedroom maisonettes (all same contact details). Breakfast and return ferry trip included in rates.

€€€-€€ Hôtel Key Largo, *19 corniche Bonaparte, T04 94 29 46 93, hotel-key-largo. com.* A pretty 18th-century former private home, midway between the Rènecros beach and Bandol's port. Rooms are decked out with bright contemporary accents or artwork; the seafront ones (eight of the 18) look out over the Ile de Bendor. There's a large ground floor terrace, and breakfast (buffet or in bed) included. No internet access to date.

€€€ Hôtel Plein Large, *Plage de Rènecros, T04 94 32 23 32, hotelpleinlarge.com.* At the eastern tip of Rènecros bay, Hôtel Plein Large offers seven simple, motel-type rooms with terraces, which face directly on to the sea. Also on site are the restaurant La Chipote and friendly snack bar/sunlounger terrace Chez Maeva. Three triples (no balconies) available too.

St-Cyr-sur-Mer *p42*

€€€€-€€€ Dolce Frégate, *Lieu-dit Frégate, Route de Bandol, T04 94 29 39 39, dolce-fregate-hotel.com.* Paradise for golf fiends, sporting two courses (9- and 18-hole, dolcefregate-golf-provence.com) plus a golf academy between Cassis and Bandol. Provençal-style rooms are airy, and there's also a spa complex, indoor and outdoor pools.

La Ciotat *p42*

€€-€ Hôtel Les Lavandes, *38 bd de la République, T04 42 08 42 81, hotel-les-lavandes.com.* This family-run, budget spot is located in downtown La Ciotat, within an easy stroll of the town's beaches. The 14 rooms are basic but clean and bright, the breakfast spread is tasty (€6.50) and there's free Wi-Fi.

Sanary-sur-Mer *p43*

€€€-€€ Hôtel de la Tour, *24 quai Général de Gaulle, T04 94 74 10 10, sanary-*

hoteldelatour.com. Sitting directly on Sanary's port, many of Hôtel de la Tour's modern, French-style rooms have harbour views. Old photos of the village line the common areas, and there's an exceptional seafood restaurant downstairs. A/C and free Wi-Fi to boot.

🍴 Restaurants

Bandol and Ile de Bendor *p41*

€€€€ Les Oliviers, *Hôtel Ile Rousse, 25 bd Louis Lumière, T04 94 29 33 00, ile-rousse. com. Daily 1200-1400 (Sep-Jun only) and 1900-2200.* Overlooking the sheltered Rènecros bay, Les Oliviers serves up some of Bandol's most refined cuisine. Menus from chef Bruno Chastagnac (€65-80) are likely to mix Mediterranean influences, such as basil *pistou* soup with Corsican sheep's cheese dumplings.

€€€€-€€€ KV&B, *5 rue de la Paroisse, T04 94 74 85 77. Mon-Sat 1200-1430 and 1930-2230.* Little sister to the well-established Le Clocher (1 rue de la Paroisse) down the road, KV&B is part trendy restaurant (crystals shimmer against the black ceiling), part very good wine bar. Menus (€12-35) are modern French; mixed plates of *charcuterie* and cheeses are also available.

€€€-€€ Le Grand Large, *Ile de Bendor, T04 94 29 81 94, restaurantgrandlarge.com. Daily 0900-1400, closed mid Nov-mid Dec.* Boasting a terrace with sea views over the Ile des Embiez (plus unusual wines from Embiez on the menu), Le Grand Large is pleasantly laid-back. Top dishes include *escargots flambés* in Ricard pastis. One of the island's few spots to remain open (almost) all year round.

€€ Pizzeria le Pinocchio, *5 rue Docteur Louis Marçon, T04 94 29 41 16. Daily 1200-1400 and 1900-2215.* Le Pinocchio's personal pizzas may weigh in around €14 each, but they're worth it. Dough is made according to a secret family recipe; pizzas are crisped in their roaring wood-fired oven. The restaurant also offers a two-course menu (€20.50, with coffee), featuring picks like Texan pork ribs or gratinéed mussels.

La Cadière d'Azur p42
€€€€ Hostellerie Bérard, *6 rue Gabriel Péri, T04 94 90 11 43, hotel-berard.com. Mid May-Oct daily 1930-2200, Wed-Sun 1200-1400, Nov-mid May Wed-Sun 1200-1400 and 1930-2200, closed Jan.* Exceptional cuisine by chefs Réne and his son Jean-François Bérard. Dinner menus range from a delectable three courses (€49) to an eight-course gourmet bonanza (€157); well-executed dishes include wild duck with caramelised beets and deconstructed *tarte tatin*. Learn how to recreate your meal at the cookery school (see What to do, below).

Entertainment

Bandol p41
Le Grand Casino de Bandol, *2 place Lucien Artaud, Bandol, T04 94 29 31 31, casinobandol.com. Daily 1100-0300.* Casino.

What to do

Bandol p41
Thalazur Bandol Thalassothérapie and Spa, *Hôtel Ile Rousse, 25 bd Louis Lumière, Bandol, T04 94 29 33 00, bandol.thalazur. fr.* Thalassotherapy, massage and skincare treatments, steps from Bandol's plage de Rènecros.

La Cadière d'Azur p42
Hostellerie Bérard Cookery School, *6 rue Gabriel Péri, La Cadière d'Azur, T04 94 90 11 43, hotel-berard.com.* Four days of market shopping, vineyard visits and cooking classes. Prices start at €1388 per person, including food and accommodation. Wine-tasting classes also available.

Transport

The towns listed in this section are all small enough to explore on foot. They are connected by buses and trains.

Bandol p41
Train station: Avenue de la Gare. Bus station: Buses depart from the bus stop in the port.

Six to ten buses per day to Sanary-sur-Mer (15 mins) and Toulon (50 mins). Frequent trains east to Sanary-sur-Mer (5 mins) and Toulon (15 mins); west to La Ciotat (10 mins), Cassis (20 mins) and Marseille (45 mins). Three to nine daily buses to Le Castellet (10 mins) and La Cadière d'Azur (15 mins).

There are six private taxis, which can be contacted through the Tourist Office or Bandol's taxi rank (T04 94 29 43 67).

Le Castellet p42
Three to nine daily buses to La Cadière d'Azur (5 mins) and Bandol (10 mins).

La Cadière d'Azur p42
Three to nine daily buses to Le Castellet (5 mins) and Bandol (15 mins).

La Ciotat p42
Frequent trains east to Bandol (10 mins), Sanary-sur-Mer (15 mins) and Toulon (25 mins); west to Cassis (10 mins) and Marseille (35 mins). Four daily buses to Cassis (15 mins).

Sanary-sur-Mer p43
Hourly buses to Toulon (35 mins). Seven to ten daily buses to Bandol (15 mins). Frequent trains east to Toulon (10 mins); west to Bandol (5 mins), La Ciotat (15 mins), Cassis (15 mins) and Marseille (50 mins).

ⓘ Directory

Bandol and around *p41*

Money ATMs along Bandol's avenue du 11 Novembre. **Medical services** Pharmacy on 1 boulevard Victor Hugo, T04 94 29 41 06. **Post office** Avenue du 11 Novembre, T36 34. **Tourist information** Allée Vivien, T04 94 29 41 35, bandol.fr (Jul-Aug daily 0900-1900, Sep-Jun Mon-Sat 0900-1200 and 1400-1800). For more information about the towns dotted around Bandol, visit their tourist office websites: **Le Castellet**, ville-lecastellet.fr; **La Cadière d'Azur**, ot-lacadieredazur.fr; **St-Cyr-sur-Mer and Les Lecques**, saintcyrsurmer.com; **La Ciotat**, tourisme-laciotat.com; **Sanary-sur-Mer**, sanarysurmer.com.

Toulon

Toulon moves to its own rhythm. Billboards advertise €25-a-night hotel rooms, the local fashion is for discount bling and there's hardly a retail chain in sight. In terms of tourism, this port city, home to France's Mediterranean navy and its megalith aircraft carrier, the *Charles de Gaulle*, is a town that time forgot. But what it does have is something lacking in its beachy neighbours: an authentic offbeat culture and a history shaped by its bustling port.

Toulon → *For listings, see pages 47-48.*

A young Napoleon Bonaparte made his name by taking charge of Toulon harbour's guns and turning them against the occupying British in 1793, a passage relived in all its nationalistic detail inside the excellent **Musée National de la Marine** ① *place Monsenergue, T04 94 02 02 01, musee-marine.fr, Jul and Aug daily 1000-1800, Sep-Jun Wed-Mon 1000-1800. €5, €4 concessions, under 25s free)*. Almost the entire French fleet was scuttled to avoid being captured by the surrounding Germans in 1942 and the city was consequently battered by Axis artillery, although the job was roundly finished off by Allied bombs a year later. The damaged city was clunkily redrawn with strangely alluring Stalin-meets-Le Corbusier blocks of flats.

Nowadays, tours run around the huge **Naval docks** from bistro-lined **quai de Cronstadt**, while *navettes* run to chilled seaside suburb of **St-Mandrier** and the beach resort of **Les Sablettes**. A few streets back, the neighbourhood known as *le Petit Chicago* is still a den of sailor bars and sexy shops, although the **Maison de la Photographie** ① *Rue Nicolas Laugier, T04 94 93 07 59, Tue-Sat 1200-1800, free*, is more in keeping with 21st century Toulon, and boutiques and bookshops are springing up around nearby place du Globe. Further west the **Hôtel des Arts** ① *236 bd Maréchal Leclerc, T04 94 91 69 18, hdatoulon.fr, free*, is an excellent contemporary art space, showcasing a range of temporary exhibitions by international and regional artists.

Toulon listings

For hotel and restaurant price codes and other relevant information, see pages 10-14.

🛏 Where to stay

Toulon *p47*
€€-€ Grand Hôtel du Dauphiné,
10 rue Berthelot, T04 94 62 16 69, grandhoteldauphine.com. Super-central classic hotel with blanket Wi-Fi, equidistant from the train station and port. Rooms have fine linen, desks, a/c and satellite on the flatscreen TVs.

🍴 Restaurants

Toulon *p47*
€€ Sidi Bou Saïd, *43 rue Jean Jaurès, T04 94 91 21 23. Mon-Sat 1200-1430 and 1900-2300.* Great North African specialist with

chic interior, complete with wacky central water feature. Tunisian specials include *brick au thon*, a deep-fried tuna and egg pocket, and spicy *salade mechouia*, along with couscous and *tajines*. Tunisian, Algerian and Moroccan wines available.

⊖ Transport

Toulon *p47*
Although Toulon is a large city, it's easy to walk to most sights of tourist interest from the train station. **Radios Taxis Toulonnais** can be reached on T04 94 93 51 51, taxi-toulon.com.

The train station is on Place de l'Europe, T36 35; the city's bus station (T04 94 24 60 00) is next door. There are seven to ten daily buses to Bandol (50 mins). Hourly buses to Sanary-sur-Mer (35 mins). Frequent trains Bandol (15 mins), Sanary-sur-Mer (10 mins), La Ciotat (25 mins), Cassis (35 mins) and Marseille (40 mins-1 hr).

❶ Directory

Toulon *p47*
Money There are plenty of ATMs, particularly along boulevard du Maréchal Leclerc. **Medical services Hôpital de Toulon Font-Pré**, 1208 av Colonel Picot, T04 04 94 61 61 61, ch-toulon.fr. **Pharmacie du Palais**, Palais Liberté, 249 boulevard du Maréchal Leclerc, T04 94 91 33 74. **Post office** Rue Prosper Ferréro, T36 31. **Tourist information** 12 place Louis Blanc, T04 94 18 53 00, toulontourisme.com (Mon, Wed-Sat 0900-1800, Jul and Aug -1900, Tue 1000-1800, Jul and Aug -1800, Apr-Oct Sun and holidays 0900-1300, Nov-Mar Sun and holidays 1000-1200).

Contents

Footprint features

Aix-en-Provence & the Lubéron

Aix-en-Provence

Aix-en-Provence (originally 'Aquae Sextiae') was founded in 122 BC when Roman troops discovered underground thermal springs. Wooed by the region's mild climate they settled down into permanent camps. A precious gem, ripe for conquest, the town bounced between ruling powers over the centuries, until reaching its 15th-century zenith under Louis II of Anjou, and his son, 'Good René'. The former established Aix's renowned university in 1409; the latter was the beloved final king of independent Provence, before the region was absorbed into the Kingdom of France.

Aix went on to grow in affluence. Archbishop Mazarin established the elegant Quartier Mazarin, and scholars and aristocrats arrived by the dozen. During the 19th century, the town nurtured the talents of one of the world's most influential artists, Paul Cézanne, as well as those of his prominent friend, novelist Emile Zola.

Today, the city remains a bastion of cultural development. Thousands of foreign students – particularly Americans – flood into Aix annually, to perfect their French or study at one of the city's many universities. The contemporary Pavillon Noir (see page 56), an award-winning glass and iron cube designed by architect Rudy Ricciotti, is home to the internationally renowned Ballet Preljocaj. Young and thriving, yet revelling in its rich history, Aix is invariably appealing.

Cours Mirabeau

Running from place du Général de Gaulle (also called La Rotonde), outside the tourist office, to the 18th-century Hôtel du Poète at its eastern end, cours Mirabeau bisects Aix's city centre. The affluent, residential Mazarin neighbourhood sits to its south, while the heart of the Old Town, criss-crossed by winding alleys and narrow roads, lies to its north. The cours' towering trees shelter pavement cafés, including **Les Deux Garçons** (see page 55), evening craft markets and ambling tourists by the dozen. It's also home to three of the city's famed fountains: Fontaine des Neuf Canons, formerly a livestock watering hole; Fontaine Moussue, a mossy fountain bubbling warm water; and Fontaine du Roi René, marked with an imposing sculpture of 'Good René'. Throughout Cézanne's childhood, the future artist lived with his family at number 55, upstairs from his father's successful *chapellerie* (hat shop). Further west on the same side of the cours, **Galerie d'Art du Conseil Général** ⓘ *21 cours Mirabeau, T04 42 93 03 67, Tue afternoon-Sun, summer 1030-1300 and 1400-1800, winter 0930-1300 and 1400-1800, free*, hosts four contemporary art shows every year, highlighting works by artists from the Bouches-du-Rhône region.

Musée Granet

ⓘ *Place St Jean de Malte, T04 42 52 88 32, museegranet-aixenprovence.fr. Tue-Sun Jun-Sep 1100-1900, Oct-May 1200-1800 (ticket desks close 1-2 hrs earlier). €4, €2 students/under 26, under 18s free, free 1st Sun of month, temporary exhibitions additional fee. Map: Aix-en-Provence, p52.*

Housed in the Eglise St-Jean-de-Malte's former priory, Musée Granet hosts an excellent range of temporary exhibitions (2009's Picasso-Cézanne show was a highlight) as well as a permanent collection comprised of modern art, 18th- and 19th-century sculpture displayed in a pale olive-toned gallery, and archaeological finds. Petite but pithy, the first floor's 'De Cézanne à Giacometti' collection includes works by Fernand Léger, Paul Klee, Giorgio Morandi and Nicolas de Staël. The museum also owns a selection of Cézanne watercolours and drawings, although these are only exhibited for three months of every year due to the artworks' fragility.

Les Thermes Sextius

ⓘ *55 av des Thermes, T04 42 23 81 82, thermes-sextius.com. Mon-Fri 0830-1930, Sat 0830-1930, Sun and hols 1030-1630. Day entrance to Fitness and Relaxation Area (pool, saunas, hammam and gym) €45, treatment packages start around €90. Map: Aix-en-Provence, p52.*

During the second century BC, Roman leader Sextius Calvinus stumbled across thermal waters bubbling up from under the earth at a balmy 34°C. Baths installed, the town of Aix was founded. The tradition continues over two millennia later. Although a small line of Roman pools are still visible outside the entrance, the bulk of the Sextius Thermal Baths are built into a mix of 18th-century mansion and a more modern complex. Drop in for a soak in the therapeutic baths, opt for 'Operation New Skin' (scrub with Camargue salt) or book a facial (Nuxe products are used). Les Thermes also run package deals with **Hôtel Aquabella** (aquabella.fr) next door.

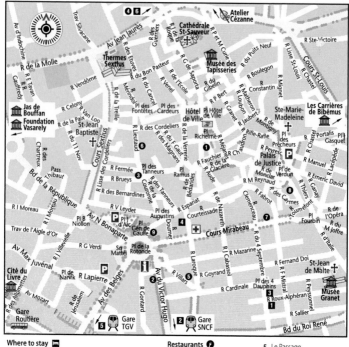

Where to stay 🛏

1 28 à Aix
2 Hôtel Cézanne
3 Hôtel des 4 Dauphins
4 Hôtel des Augustins
5 Hôtel Le Pigonnet
6 Hôtel Paul

Restaurants 🍴

1 Bar Brigand
2 Brasserie Léopold
3 Le Cantine Végétarienne
4 Le Clos de la Violette
5 Le Passage
6 Le Zinc d'Hugo
7 Les Deux Garçons
8 Restaurant Pierre Reboul
9 Simply Food

Cathédrale St-Sauveur

ⓘ *Place Martyrs de la Résistance, cathedrale-aixenprovence-monument.fr. Daily 0730-1200 and 1400-1800. Free. Map: Aix-en-Provence, p52.*

Sitting at the heart of Aix's Old Town, the Cathédrale St-Sauveur was built over a period of close to 1300 years. The cathedral's history is neatly reflected in its mix of architectural styles: Roman and Gothic gates, and its three naves (Roman, Gothic and Baroque). Head inside for a peek at both the 18th-century organ and Nicolas Froment's recently restored masterpiece, *The Burning Bush*. Adjacent are the cathedral's cloisters, its courtyard lined with ornately carved columns.

Musée des Tapisseries

ⓘ *Ancien Palais de l'Archevêché, 28 place des Martyrs de la Résistance, T04 42 23 09 91. Wed-Mon mid Apr-mid Oct 1000-1800, mid Oct-mid Apr 1330-1700. €3.20. Map: Aix-en-Provence, p52.*

The Archbishop's former palace is the unique setting for this collection of 17th- and 18th-century tapestries. The museum opened in 1909, but it was only in 1979 that contemporary textiles were included; it now also organises temporary exhibitions of modern art, and has a wing dedicated to the history of the annual **Festival International d'Art Lyrique** (festival-aix.com).

Cité du Livre

ⓘ *Bibliothèque Méjanes, 8-10 rue des Allumettes, T04 42 91 98 88, citedulivre-aix.com. Tue-Sat 1000-1900. Map: Aix-en-Provence, p52.*

A cultural centre located in an old match factory, with the Méjanes Library at its core. The Cité du Livre offers a lively monthly programme of art house films in original language, lyric art and filmed opera showings (usually free), plus children's workshops.

Atelier Cézanne

ⓘ *9 av Paul Cézanne, T04 42 21 06 53, atelier-cezanne.com. Jul-Aug 1000-1800, tour (English) 1700, Apr-Jun and Sep 1000-1200 and 1400-1800, tour (English) 1700, Oct-Mar 1000-1200 and 1400-1700, tour (English) 1600. €5.50, €2 under 25s, under 12s free. Bus no 1 to 'Paul Cézanne'. Map: Aix-en-Provence, p52.*

A brisk 10-minute hike out of town, Cézanne's final *atelier*, and the rambling gardens that surround it, are well worth the (uphill) effort needed to arrive as the artist did every day, on foot.

Two years after his mother's death, Cézanne was forced to sell the family home, Jas de Bouffan. With the proceeds, he purchased this plot of land on Les Lauves hill in 1901, designed his own studio and had it purpose-built. He came here daily, following a strict painting schedule (0600-1030, lunch in Aix, straight back to the studio until 1700) until his death in 1906.

The northern side of the 50-sq-m studio is one massive wall of glass, while the southern has two large windows, in order to allow as much natural light into the room as possible. As the 19th century petered to a close, painting nude models al fresco was still a social no-no; the studio's swathes of natural light allowed Cézanne to create the perfect conditions to complete his unfinished *Grandes Baigneuses* and other masterpieces.

Post Cézanne's death, the studio remained closed for 15 years. Marcel Provence, who purchased the building and its land in 1921, kept everything just how he found it. And happily so: today, it's possible to see the very wine bottles, chairs, pitchers, fruit stands, skulls and an armless statue of a toddler that feature in some of Cézanne's most famous artworks, as well as the artist's coat, hat and personal photos. French- and English-speaking staff are on hand to answer questions.

Jas de Bouffan

ⓘ *17 route de Galice, T04 42 16 11 91. Jun-Sep tours (45 mins) at 1030, 1200, 1400 (in English) and 1530, Apr-May and Oct Tue, Thu and Sat tours at 1030, 1200, 1400 (in English) and 1530, Nov-Mar Wed and Sat 1000-1045 (one tour only). €5.50, €2 under 25s, under 12s free. Bus no 6 to 'Corsy'. Map: Aix-en-Provence, p52.*

This sprawling 18th-century mansion was the Cézanne family home from 1870 to 1899. Cézanne used one of the spacious ground floor rooms as his studio, and it was here that he painted 12 of his masterpieces directly on to the walls (since removed and transferred to various museums). From his out door easel, Cézanne turned his attention to the house and grounds, depicting it in over 50 artworks. Note that Jas de Bouffan can only be visited on one of the scheduled tours.

Les carrières de Bibémus (Bibémus quarries)

ⓘ *Chemin de Bibémus, T04 42 16 11 91. English tours: Sat 1000; French tours: Jun-Sep 0945-1045 (one tour only, 1 hr), Apr-May and Oct Mon, Wed, Fri and Sun 1030 and 1530, Nov-Mar Wed and Sat 1500-1600 (one tour only). €6.60, €3.10 under 25s, under 12s €1.10, entrance includes return ticket for the shuttle bus (obligatory transport to quarries from 3 Bons Dieux car park). Bus no 4 to '3 Bons Dieux'. Map: Aix-en-Provence, p52.*

During the 1890s, Cézanne rented a tiny house in the abandoned Bibémus stone quarries. The orange, blocky paintings he created here during this period are generally heralded as precursors to the Cubist movement of the early 20th century. Note that a trip to the Bibémus quarries may be most appealing to those who enjoy an out-of-town ramble, as opposed to art enthusiasts. Visits can only be undertaken on one of the scheduled tours; comfortable walking shoes are advised.

Fondation Vasarely

ⓘ *1 av Marcel Pagnol, Jas de Bouffan, T04 42 20 01 09, fondationvasarely.fr. Tue-Sat 1000-1300 and 1400-1800. €9, €6 7-26 years, €4 3-7 years, under 3s free, free audioguide. Bus nos 4 or 6 to 'Fondation Vasarely'. Map: Aix-en-Provence, p52.*

Through the 1940s and '50s, Hungarian-born artist Victor Vasarely's spiral swirls and geometrical patterns of black, white and solid colours helped establish the optical art, or op art, movement.

Provence had long been a favourite region for Vasarely. Although he lived near Paris, his summer holidays were spent in Gordes; the artist even established his first museum (now closed) in the hilltop town's 16th-century castle. From 1971, Vasarely designed and planned the construction and layout of his Fondation; in 1973 the Aix-en-Provence municipality donated land to the artist for its creation, and construction began. The Fondation was finally inaugurated in 1976.

Over the 30 years since its opening, the museum has been fraught with drama, from leaky roofs to artworks siphoned on to the black market by a former Fondation director. Still a treat, on the ground floor seven rooms ('hexagonal cells') display Vasarely's 42 giant 'architectural integrations' beneath their 11-m ceilings. The museum also stages temporary exhibitions.

Aix-en-Provence listings

For hotel and restaurant price codes and other relevant information, see pages 10-14.

☐ Where to stay

Aix-en-Provence *p51, map p52*

€€€€ 28 à Aix, *28 rue du 4 Septembre, T04 42 54 82 01, 28-a-aix.com.* Modern and elegant, 28 à Aix, a 17th-century townhouse opened in 2008 by the founders of Villa Gallici (a luxury hotel just outside Aix's centre, T04 42 23 29 23, villagallici.com). All four suites are sumptuous: Suite 1 features a four-poster bed draped in luxury linens, Suite 3 a private terrace overlooking Aix's rooftops. Two nights minimum.

€€€€ Hôtel Cézanne, *40 av Victor Hugo, T04 42 91 11 11, cezanne.hotelaix.com.* Hip Hôtel Cézanne touts itself as the city's only boutique option. Bright colours and animal prints grace the ground floor common areas, while bedrooms are more neutral, but just as funky. There's an honesty bar, plus a free guest car park around the corner.

€€€€ Hôtel Le Pigonnet, *5 av du Pigonnet, T04 42 59 02 90, hotelpigonnet.com.* Less than a kilometre from downtown Aix, Le Pigonnet's position allows guests to relax far from the crowds, yet easily explore the city sights by foot. Gardens, including a pool, are rambling and lush; Cézanne reputedly painted Mount Ste-Victoire from here. Rates can range from bargain to steep, depending on the season and room category.

€€€-€€ Hôtel des Augustins, *3 rue de la Masse, T04 42 27 28 59, hotel-augustins. com.* Formerly a 12th-century convent, Hôtel des Augustins claims Martin Luther as its most famous guest: the father of Protestantism temporarily resided here in 1521, post excommunication by Pope Leo X. The 29 atmospheric rooms mix monastic decor with Provençal prints and more luxurious trimmings.

€€ Hôtel des 4 Dauphins, *54 rue Roux Alphéran, T04 42 38 16 39, lesquatredauphins. fr.* Thirteen petite rooms, down the street from the Quatre Dauphins fountain. Decor has been chosen with attention to detail, keeping an authentic Provençal theme throughout. Although only a five-minute walk from the town's bustling centre, the hotel's position in residential Quartier Mazarin means evenings are quiet year round.

€ Hôtel Paul, *10 av Pasteur, T04 42 23 23 89, aix-en-provence.com/hotelpaul.* Hôtel Paul lies north of the Old Town, just beyond Cathédrale St-Sauveur. Tiny, basic and very friendly, the hotel is decorated with giant Cézanne prints (the artist's Atelier, see page 53, is up the road). Rooms are all en suite, and there's a shady garden for breakfast (€5).

🍴 Restaurants

Aix-en-Provence *p51, map p52*
€€€€ Le Clos de la Violette, *10 av de la Violette, T04 42 23 30 71, closdelaviolette.com. Tue-Sat 1200-1330 and 1930-2130.* Michelin-starred cuisine in a pretty garden, just north of Aix's Old Town. Jean-Marc Banzo's market-based set menu (€50, not served Sun) changes daily; other set menus (€90 and €130) are seasonal.

€€€€ Restaurant Pierre Reboul, *11 petite rue St Jean, T04 42 20 58 26, restaurant-pierre-reboul.com. Tue-Sat 1200-1330 and 1930-2130.* Creating edible *trompe l'œil* since opening in 2007, Pierre Reboul's molecular masterpieces have earned him a Michelin star. Nothing is what is seems, from Munster cheese profiteroles to his famous 'fried egg' (mango and biscuit) dessert. Menus €42-142.

€€€ Brasserie Léopold, *2 av Victor Hugo, T04 42 26 01 24, hotel-saintchristophe. com. Daily 1200-1500 and 1900-2400.* Waiters in waistcoats bustle past red leather banquettes at this unpretentious brasserie. Although you'll find classics such as steak tartare, dishes are also innovative: *magret de canard* is minced with honey and figs, artichokes are paired with sweet broad beans.

€€€-€€ Les Deux Garçons, *53 cours Mirabeau, T04 42 26 00 51, les2garconsrestaurant.com. Daily 1200-2300.* An 18th-century institution, favoured by Cézanne and Zola. The menu focuses mostly on seafood, although plenty of locals pop in for a sandwich and a *pression*. Service can be patchy.

€€€-€€ Le Passage, *10 rue Villars, T04 42 37 09 00, le-passage.fr. Daily 1000-2400, restaurant 1130-1430 and 1930-2330.* Housed in an old factory, Le Passage includes a restaurant, deli, seafood specialist, wine shop and cooking school. Expect excellent value set menus (a two-course lunch plus glass of wine is €13) and jazz with your evening aperitif. Fun and young.

€€€ Le Zinc d'Hugo, *22 rue Lieutaud, T04 42 27 69 69, zinc-hugo.com. Tue-Sat 1200-1430 and 1900-2230, closed mid Jul-mid Aug.* Chef Christophe Formeau trained as a *charcutier* (pork butcher) in Paris; it's no surprise Le Zinc's menu is littered with homemade terrines, pâté and sausages. The rustic ambiance lends itself well to the wood-fired meats, duck, beef, lamb and pork included.

€ La Cantine Végétarienne, *Place des Tanneurs, T06 13 46 02 16. Mon-Sat 1130-1500.* This cosy cafe and restaurant – its decor all natural wood and hand-blown coloured glass – dishes up a daily buffet of veggie and vegan delights: fill your boots for €14.50. Add another €3 to sample their freshly-baked desserts. Also a great stop for tea and homemade cake (€3).

Cafés and bars
Bar Brigand, *17 place Richelme, T04 42 12 46 81. Mon-Sat 0900-0200, Sun 1400-0200.* Offering an unbeatable 40-plus beers. During happy hour (1830-2030) pints are €3.50 each.

Simply Food, *67 rue Espariat, T04 42 59 52 85, simply-food.fr. Mon-Sat 0900-1900.* Fresh, speedy and often organic meals to take away or eat on the small terrace. Salads include barley, edamame beans, goat's cheese and hazelnuts (€3.90) and there's always a soup of the day (€3.50).

Entertainment

Aix-en-Provence *p51, map p52*
Clubs
Mistral Club, *3 rue Frédéric Mistral, T04 42 38 16 49, mistralclub.fr. Tue-Sat 2400-late.* Resident DJs pack the house with electro, techno and occasionally 80s tunes.

Theatre
Pavillon Noir, *530 av Mozart, T04 42 93 48 80, preljocaj.org.* Contemporary performances by the excellent Ballet Preljocaj. From 2013, the new Kengo Kuma-designed Conservatoire will stage concerts next door.

Shopping

Aix-en-Provence *p51, map p52*
Art
Boutique des Musées, *5 rue des Chaudronniers, T04 42 23 46 44, boutiquesdemusees.fr. Tue-Sat 1000-1230 and 1430-1900.* Pick up small artwork replicas – from a Degas dancer to sparkling sculptures by Niki de Saint Phalle – found in French museums.

Books
Book in bar, *4 rue Joseph Cabassol, T04 42 26 60 07, bookinbar.com. Mon-Sat 0900-1900.* Combo English bookstore and cosy coffee shop.

Clothes
Papa Pique et Maman Coud, *31 rue Bédarrides, T04 42 26 64 54, papapiqueetmamancoud.com. Jul-Aug Mon-Sat 1000-2000; Sep-Jul Mon 1400-1900, Tue-Sat 1000-1900.* Southern outpost of this playful Brittany-based brand, selling bags, barrettes and children's clothes.

L'Étoile de Montmartre, *39 rue des Cordeliers, T04 86 31 53 34, etoiledemontmartre.com. Tue-Sat 1200-1900.* Starry T-shirts, Japanese-inspired tops and made-to-order wedding dresses, created by designer Rosalie in her atelier behind the shop.

Food and drink
Calissons du Roy René, *13 rue Gaston de Saporta, T04 42 26 67 86, calisson.com. Mon-Sat 0930-1300 and 1400-1830, Sun 1000-1600.* Purveyors of Aix's famous candied fruit *calisson*. Pop into the basement to check out their dedicated museum (free).

Souvenirs
Décalé, *14 rue d'Italie, T04 42 53 32 65. Tue-Sat 1000-1230 and 1400-1900.* Ultra-design teapots, mobiles, beaded bags and cushion covers printed with city skylines.

Aix-en-Provence *p51, map p52*
Cultural
Aix-en-Provence City Tours, *Office de Tourisme, Les allées provençales, 300 av Giuseppe Verdi, Aix-en-Provence, T04 42 16 11 61, aixenprovencetourism.com. Apr-Oct Tue and Sat 1000, Nov-Mar Sat 1000. €8, €4 concessions, under 6s free.* Two-hour English-language tours of Aix's Old Town.
In the steps of Cézanne, *Office de Tourisme, Les allées provençales, 300 av Giuseppe Verdi, Aix-en-Provence, T04 42 16 11 61, aixenprovencetourism.com. Apr-Oct Thu 1000. €8, €4 concessions, under 6s free.* English-language tours charting Cézanne's life in Aix (approx 2 hrs).

Aix-en-Provence *p51, map p52*
Walking is the easiest way to get around the city, as the Old Town is compact, with most points of interest no more than 20 minutes apart by foot. Buses (aixenbus.fr) for Aix sights outside the centre depart from La Rotonde (place du Général de Gaulle), near the tourist office. Tickets (€1) can be purchased on board. There are taxi stands at the bus and train stations; alternatively contact the Association Taxis Radio Aixois (T04 42 27 71 11, taxisradioaixois.com) for pick-up.

The train stations are **TGV**: RD 9, plateau de l'Arbois (T08 92 35 35 35, tgv.com); **SNCF**: rue Gustave Desplaces (T36 35, voyages-sncf.com). Trains to Manosque every two hours (45 mins).

The bus station is on Avenue de l'Europe, (T08 21 20 22 03, lepilote.com). Frequent shuttles (*navettes*) operate between the TGV and bus stations (20 mins, €3.60, tickets can be purchased on board). There are one

to four buses per day to Lourmarin (1 hr), Bonnieux (1hr 25) and Apt (1hr 45).

Aix-en-Provence *p51, map p52*
Money There are plenty of ATMs dotted throughout the city, including seven along cours Mirabeau. **Medical services Centre Hospitalier du Pays d'Aix**, avenue des Tamaris, T04 42 33 50 00, ch-aix.fr. Pharmacy at 17bis cours Mirabeau, T04 42 93 63 60.
Post office Place de l'Hôtel de Ville, T04 42 17 10 41. **Tourist information** 2 Les allées provençales, 300 av Giuseppe Verdi, T04 42 16 11 61, aixenprovencetourism. com (Mon-Sat 0830-1900, Sun 1000-1300 and 1400-1800, Jul-Aug extended hours). Buy an **Aix City Pass** (€15, available from the tourist office, valid for five days) for free entry to four major sights, tours of the Atelier Cézanne and Jas de Bouffan, a city tour (see What to do, above) and a free loop around the city on Le Petit Tourist Train (cpts.fr). If you plan to visit Cézanne's Atelier, Jas de Bouffan and the Bibémus Quarries, purchase the discounted **Cézanne Pass** (€12), which allows one entry into each of the three sites, and is valid for the calendar year. Note that the return ticket for the Bibémus quarries shuttle bus (€1.10, obligatory transport to quarries from 3 Bons Dieux car park) is not included in the pass. (Also note that you can follow the trail of 'C' brass studs embedded in the city's pavements: these will take you around town to the spots where Cézanne used to live and work.) The **Aix et le Pays d'Aix pass** (Pass for Aix and Aix Countryside, aixenprovencetourism.com, €2, available from the tourist office) will entitle the holder to free or discounted entry to museums (including Musée Granet and Fondation Vasarely), vineyards, concerts, tours and transport in and around Aix.

The Lubéron

Perhaps best known for its starring role in the film and novel, *A Good Year*, the region rolling north of Aix-en-Provence barely breaks a metaphorical sweat, so effortlessly does it attract visitors by the busload. The *villages perchés* (hilltop villages), enchanting ochre cliffs, vineyards, sunflowers and especially the lavender – come July it's purple as far as the eye can see – are trumpeted by their supporters as an antithesis to glitzier towns dotted along the Mediterranean coast.

Yet the Lubéron and its environs have long been favoured by escaping expats and famous French: Samuel Beckett, Albert Camus, Picasso and Dora Maar, John Malkovich, Ridley Scott and Pierre Cardin, among so many others, all chose to make this area their (sometimes second) home. The region isn't 'undiscovered', but that doesn't negate that there is indeed something magical about the postcard-perfect countryside around here: get off the main tourist trails and you'll soon find it.

Note that the Lubéron is poorly connected by public transport. If you choose to bed down out of town, it's wise to ensure your hotel has an on-site restaurant (and that it's open). After a busy day sightseeing, all you may be up for is tucking into a rack of local Sisteron lamb, then tucking yourself up into bed.

Gordes → *For listings, see pages 62-66.*

The archetypical Provençal perched village of Gordes soars above the undulating vineyards and fields of lavender that gather at its base. Buildings of the palest golden stone clamber perilously atop each other: the town is almost more scenic from afar than within, not least because you're still a peaceful distance from its (often) tourist-clogged streets.

At the heart of Gordes' town centre sits its 16th-century **château**, which has been used alternatively as a prison, barracks, post office and boys' school. Between 1970 and 1996, the castle housed a museum dedicated to Victor Vasarely. This same space is now home to the **Musée Pol Mara** ① *entrance place Genty Pantaly, T04 90 72 02 75, daily 1000-1200 and 1400-1800, €4, €3 child (10-17), under 10s free* – the Belgian contemporary artist was a former resident of the village – and the **tourist office** ① *T04 90 72 02 75, gordes-village. com*. The pretty square out front, place Genty Pantaly, featured in Ridley Scott's 2006 film *A Good Year* (based on Mayle's book), as did the hotel and restaurant **La Renaissance** (see page 63).

Heading downhill, peek inside the richly painted Eglise de St-Firmin, before continuing on to the **Caves du Palais St Firmin** ① *rue du Belvédère, May-Sep daily 1000-1800, €5, €4 students/under 17s*, stone cellars that burrow beneath a former noble home and demonstrate old-style manual agricultural tasks, such as making olive oil. Near the cellars' entrance, there are stunning panoramic views over the Théâtre des Terrasses (occasional site of the town's annual Les Soirées d'Eté de Gordes) and the valley below.

Space allowing, it's best to park at the car park above place du Château (direction Murs); the lower car park (nearest the turn off for the Abbaye de Sénanque, direction Venasque) requires a steep hike uphill to the town centre.

Abbaye Notre-Dame de Sénanque

① *RD 177, route de Venasque, T04 90 72 05 72, abbayedesenanque.com. Grounds always open, access to interior by guided visit only (in French, 50 visitors max per tour, 1 hr). Tours: Jul-Aug Mon-Sat 1010 and 1030, daily 1430, 1450, 1510, 1530, 1545, 1600, 1615 and 1630; Jun and Sep Mon-Sat 1010 and 1030, daily 1430, 1510, 1530, 1610 and 1630; May Mon-Sat 1010 and 1030, daily 1430, 1530 and 1630; Feb-Apr and Oct-mid Nov Mon-Sat 1030, daily 1430, 1530 and 1630; mid Nov-Jan daily 1450 and 1620; Boutique: Feb-mid Nov Mon-Sat 1000-1800, Sun 1400-1800; mid Nov-Jan daily 1400-1800; closed 2 weeks in Jan. €7, €5 students/ under 25s, €3 child (6-18), under 6s free.*

Set in a bucolic valley 4 km from Gordes, this Cistercian abbey was built in 1148 and has been religiously active ever since. The grounds are always open to the public: wander through the lavender fields or circle around the back for a peek at the resident monks' vegetable gardens. Join one of the abbey's guided tours in order to visit the monks' former dormitory, the Abbey church, cloisters and 'scriptorium' (where manuscripts were transcribed). The Abbaye also welcomes individuals for spiritual retreats (max 8 days, approx €30/day, frere.hotelier@senanque.fr for further information).

Note that clothing and behaviour should be appropriate to the strict religious setting. The on-site boutique sells the abbey's own honey and lavender products.

Village des Bories

① *West of Gordes, direction Cavaillon, T04 90 72 03 48. Daily 0900-sunset. €6, €4 child (12-17), under 12s free.*

Bories – unusual, often conical drystone dwellings – can be found all over Provence. Rather than primary residences, *bories* were enclosed, functional spaces: storerooms for agricultural tools, shelter for a shepherd's flock, outdoor kitchens or even houses for silkworm farms.

This cluster of 30 or so huts is the largest grouping in the region. Abandoned over a hundred years ago, these *bories* were built any time between the seventh and 19th centuries; they were heavily restored between 1969 and 1976, then declared a protected site in 1977. Visitors can also stop in at the small museum dedicated to dry-stone architecture at the entrance to the village.

Musée de la Lavande

① *Route de Gordes, Coustellet, T04 90 76 91 23, museedelalavande.com. Daily May-Sep 0900-1900, Feb-Apr and Oct-Dec 0900-1215 and 1400-1800, closed Jan, ticket desks close 30 mins earlier. €6.50, €5.50 students, under 15s free if accompanied by paying adult, free audioguide.*
A shrine to the fragrant purple blossom for which the Lubéron is so famous. Owned by **Le Château du Bois** (espritlavande.eu), an 80-ha estate producing 10% of France's lavender, the museum charts the history and current production methods used for harvesting the plant's essential oil. It also houses a huge collection of copper stills (used for distilling lavender oil), as well as antique perfume bottles and traditional local costumes. On your way out, stock up on all things lavender – soap, candles, tea and honey – at the on-site boutique.

Roussillon → *For listings, see pages 62-66.*

Long renowned for its ochre deposits, deep red and yellow-based pigments found in the clay of the immediate area, Roussillon remains a vision of glowing sunset hues. The village's hilltop houses range from amber to russet, the colours intensified against a backdrop of dark oak forests and rolling vineyards.

Ochre can be used to dye anything from textiles to cosmetics, and mining for the local pigments peaked in the 1920s. Less than three decades later, the town's foundations were in danger of collapsing due to the avid mining, and activity soon ground to a halt.

Explore the former quarries along **Le Sentier des Ocres de Roussillon** ① *Ochre Footpath, entrance signposted a 5-min walk from the town centre, daily Jul-Aug 0900-1930, Jun 0900-1830, May and Sep 0930-1830, Apr 0930-1730, Oct 0930-1630, Mar 0930-1700, first 2 weeks Nov 1000-1630, mid Nov-Dec and last 3 weeks Feb 1100-1530, closed Jan-first week Feb, €2.50, joint ticket Usine Mathieu and Sentier des Ocres €7, under 10s free; short walk 35 mins, long walk 50 mins.* Or head 1.5 km out of town to the **Ancienne Usine Mathieu** ① *RD104, T04 90 05 66 69, okhra.com, Jul-Aug daily 0900-1900, Feb-Jun and Sep-Nov daily 0900-1800, Dec-Jan Wed-Sun 0900-1800, €6, joint ticket as above, under 10s free,* a former ochre factory, where visitors can see how the pigments were washed, processed and transformed from earthen clay to dye.

Bonnieux → *For listings, see pages 62-66.*

A hilltop village crowded with cobblestone streets, antique stores and pavement cafés, Bonnieux's panoramic vistas (best seen from near the old church) are 'a terrace overlooking the world' according to one overheard visitor. Bonnieux also boasts the quirky **Musée de la Boulangerie** ① *12 rue de la République, T04 90 75 88 34, Wed-Mon Jul-Aug 1000-1300 and 1400-1800, Apr-Jun and Sep-Oct 1000-1230 and 1430-1800, €3.50, €1.50 students/child*

Five of the best Provençal markets

Any of the following markets are an excellent source of delicious local fruits and vegetables, cheese, *charcuterie*, olives, honey and nougat. You'll also find organic essential oils, soaps and pottery. In addition, look out for Cavaillon's famous melons (which are available in July) and truffles from the hills around Apt (which are available from November–March).

Cavaillon Place du Clos, Monday mornings.
Vaison-la-Romaine Throughout the town centre, Tuesday mornings. See over page.
Lourmarin Place Henri Barthélémy, Friday mornings.
Manosque Place Marcel Pagnol, Saturday mornings.
Apt Place de la Bouquerie and around, Saturday mornings.

(12-16)/over 60, under 12s free, which traces the cultivation of wheat, the process of refining flour and various methods of baking.

North of the town, heading towards Apt, don't miss the 2000-year-old **Pont Julien** spanning the Calavon River. The dry-stone bridge is part of the old Via Domitia, the principal Roman trade route between Italy and the Iberian Peninsula. The bridge is accessible by bike and on foot; it's also visible from the D108 that runs parallel past it.

Lacoste

In 2001, fashion tycoon Pierre Cardin purchased Lacoste's medieval castle, formerly the residence of the infamous Marquis de Sade. The castle, under slow restoration, is used in part for the town's annual **Festival d'Art Lyrique et de Théâtre de Lacoste** ① *Jul-Aug, festivaldelacoste.com*, and its views, to Bonnieux and beyond, are well worth the hike. However, Cardin's long-term plans for the town have proved controversial: he intends to create a 'cultural St-Tropez', snapping up (in some estimates) close to 40 village homes for his project, paying around twice their market value. His critics accuse Cardin of stifling the community, transforming the town into a cluster of desolate streets. Visit out of season and their comments ring painfully true.

The town is also home to a branch of the Savannah College of Art and Design (scad.edu); temporary installations of artwork are frequently dotted around the village.

Lourmarin → *For listings, see pages 62-66.*

Oh-so-pretty Lourmarin ticks all the boxes: pretty winding alleys, Provençal shops stocked with local wine and linens, and plenty of terraces, perfect for lingering over a glass of rosé. The town boasts one of the region's best weekly **markets** (see box, above), although its main cultural draw is the Renaissance **Château de Lourmarin** ① *T04 90 68 15 23, chateau-de-lourmarin.com, daily Jun-Aug 1000-1800, May and Sep 1030-1130 and 1430-1730, Mar-Apr and Oct 1030-1130 and 1430-1630, Feb and Nov-Dec 1030-1130 and 1430-1600, Jan Sat 1030-1130 and 1430-1600, Sun 1030-1130, €6, €3.50 students, €2.50 child (10-16), under 10s free*, located a five-minute walk west of the village and surrounded by olive trees. The Château houses a collection of antique furniture, musical instruments and prints.

Lourmarin's most famous resident was Algerian-born author Albert Camus, who lived in the town during the last years of his life; his remains are buried in the town cemetery.

Vaison-la-Romaine

Lying in the Vaucluse's northern region, approximately 50km north of Gordes, the market town of Vaison-la-Romaine (vaison-ventoux-tourisme.com) makes an appealing day out for visitors with their own transport. Stroll through Vaison's superb Roman sites, Puymin and Villasse, its amphitheatre or cross the Ouvèze River by a bridge from the same period. Head up to the medieval Haute-Ville for fabulous views over Mont Ventoux and the valleys below.

The Lubéron listings

For hotel and restaurant price codes and other relevant information, see pages 10-14.

🛏 Where to stay

Note that because the Lubéron is dotted with myriad petite, picturesque villages, many of the listings below are located in towns that haven't been mentioned elsewhere in this guide. However, all are within easy driving distance of the region's most popular sights.

Gordes *p59*
€€€€ Hôtel Les Bories, *Route de l'Abbaye de Sénanque, T04 90 72 00 51, hotellesbories. com*. Craving physical immersion in all that fragrant lavender? Guests at this sumptuous spot can take advantage of La Maison d'Ennea (see page 65), the on-site spa, as well as indoor and outdoor pools, tennis court and chef Pascal Ginoux's fine dining. Although the 31 luxury rooms and two apartments are pricey, the hotel often offers packages; check online.
€€€-€€ La Ferme de la Huppe, *RD 156, Les Pourquiers, T04 90 72 12 25, lafermedelahuppe.com*. Ten airy, pale-stone bedrooms are dotted around this 18th-century *bastide*; each one retains the name of its former function, such as L'Ecurie (stables) or La Cuisine (kitchen). A few kilometres outside the tourist haven of Gordes, the hotel also has a pretty outdoor pool trimmed by lush vegetation. Note that

the excellent on-site restaurant is closed between November and mid-March.

Les Gros
€€€ Le Moulin des Sources, *Les Gros, T04 90 72 11 69, le-moulin-des-sources.com*. More a cushy stay with friends than a standard B&B, just outside Gordes. Peeking out over the pool and olive trees, Geneviève and Gérard's five en suite rooms are decked out in sophisticated grey. Once a week, Gérard cooks up a communal feast (€35 per person, including aperitif, wine and coffee), served in the garden or alongside the kitchen's open fire. No TV; limited English.

Les Beaumettes
€€ Au Ralenti du Lierre, *Village des Beaumettes, T04 90 72 39 22, auralentidulierre. com*. A lovely B&B between Ménerbes and Gordes, managed by the gregarious Thierry. High-ceilinged bedrooms blend Provençal greens, blues and reds with wooden *armoires* and wrought iron chairs. Breakfast breads, pastries and jams are home-made, and there's a fabulous pool and garden out back. Guests benefit from both Au Ralenti's intimacy and its superb village location.

Bonnieux *p60*
€€€€-€€€ Auberge de l'Aiguebrun, *Domaine de la Tour, T04 90 04 47 00, aubergedelaiguebrun.fr. Closed Nov-Mar*. Four kilometres outside Bonnieux's town centre, Auberge de l'Aiguebrun is a perfect

hideaway. Dip into the pool, dine at the divine restaurant (closed Mon-Wed out of season) or simply sprawl on one of the canopied garden beds. More private are the two-person wooden chalets (€€€), built alongside a woodland stream.

Lourmarin *p61*

€€€ Le Moulin du Lourmarin, *Rue de Temple, T04 90 68 06 69, moulindelourmarin. com*. Le Moulin's previous incarnation – as an 18th-century olive oil mill – is easily envisioned within the hotel's cavernous foyer. Airy and open, a contemporary glass lift whizzes guests up to the 19 pretty rooms, while an open fire blazes downstairs in winter. The hotel also houses a bakery and a small boutique. Breakfast included.

Les Olivettes, *Av Henri Bosco, T04 90 68 03 52, olivettes.com*. Six studio and one-bedroom apartments, individually decorated and comfortably stocked, within a large Provençal farmhouse. Friendly owners Elisabeth and Joe are on hand to help guests plan outings and pick restaurants. Rentals available by the week during high season (€950-1860, sleeping 2-4), and by the week or month (heavily discounted) from Nov-Feb; pets are welcome.

Manosque

€€ Le Pré Saint Michel, *435 montée de la Mort d'Imbert, T04 92 72 14 27, presaintmichel.com*. Delightfully off the tourist track, Le Pré's tasteful rooms (superior ones with private terraces) have views over the countryside and very welcome swimming pool. A buffet breakfast is served on the sundeck; bathrooms are stocked with L'Occitane products, fresh from the factory down the road (see page 65). La Table du Pré Saint Michel (see page 64) next door offers half-board options.

Saignon

€€ Chambre de Séjour avec Vue – Demeure d'art et d'hôtes, *Les sablières, T04 90 04 85 01, chambreavecvue.com*. Part B&B, part art gallery, Chambre de Séjour avec Vue (room with a view) is a bright, eclectic mix of colours and contemporary creations. The three intimate rooms share access to a communal living room, dining room (both with open fireplaces) and garden. Owners Pierre and Kamila are welcoming, helpful and very knowledgeable, both about local art and the region.

🍴 Restaurants

Gordes *p59*

€€-€ L'Encas, *Place du Château, T04 90 72 29 82. Daily 1200-1430 and 1900-2200, closed Nov*. Pick of the in-town eateries, with quality *plats du jour*, like beef *entrecôte* with homemade chips (€12), and giant salads (from €10). In the small dining room, head for the two tables at the back, which have great views.

Cafés and bars

La Renaissance, *Place Genty Pantaly, T04 90 72 02 02. Daily 1000-2200, closed Nov*. Best savoured mid-afternoon, with a scoop of divine organic sorbet (€6). Also an overpriced restaurant, featured in the film *The Good Life*.

Grambois

€€€ L'Auberge des Tilleuls, *Moulin du Pas, T04 90 77 93 11, tilleuls.com. Jul-Aug daily 1200-1400 and 1930-2130, Sep-Dec and Feb-Jun Wed-Sun 1200-1400 and 1930-2130*. With a terrace tucked under lime trees (*tilleuls*), this lovely old restaurant – under the direction of chef Dominique Bucaille – dishes up simple, yet traditional Provençal cuisine. Look out for the melt-in-your-mouth Sisteron lamb but save room for the exquisite desserts, prepared by Dominique's daughter Julia.

Roussillon *p60*

€€€€ Restaurant David, *Le Clos de la Glycine, place de la Poste*, T04 90 05 60 13, luberon-hotel.com. *May-Oct daily 1200-1400 and 1930-2200, Nov-Apr Mon 1930-2200, Tue and Thu-Sat 1200-1400 and 1930-2200, Sun 1200-1400, closed mid Nov-mid Dec and mid Jan-mid Feb.* Sample chef Emmanuel Champion's seasonal creations on the panoramic terrace, against a backdrop of ochre cliffs. Of particular note is the red mullet, served with butternut squash ravioli and leek, potato and morel mushroom sauce (€29) and the partridge salame, dished up with heirloom veggie casserole and spicy beet chips (€28). Menus €35, €50 and €55.

Bonnieux *p60*
€€€-€€ L'Arôme Restaurant,
2 rue Lucien Blanc, T04 90 75 88 62, larome-restaurant.com. *Apr-Dec Fri-Mon 1230-1400 and 1930-2130, Thu 1930-2130.* Southern French cuisine, served up in the 14th-century vaulted dining room or on the terrace. Owned by chef Jean-Michel Pages and maître d' Clara, the restaurant also has an extensive *cave à vins* (wine cellar) and always offers a special wine by the glass (€5).

Cucuron
€€€€ La Petite Maison de Cucuron,
Place de l'Étang, T04 90 68 21 99, lapetitemaisondecucuron.com. *Wed-Sun 1200-1400 and 2000-2130.* Chef Eric Sapet reopened this charming restaurant back in 2007, and now serves just two weekly menus (priced at €46 and €68). Flavours are sophisticated – for example, pork roast with a walnut crust, or turbot with capers, lemon and toasted pine nuts. Foodies also flock to Chef Sapet's renowned cooking classes (€68 including lunch), which often build a menu around one seasonal ingredient.

Lourmarin *p61*
€€€-€€ La Récréation, *15 av Philippe de Girard*, T04 90 68 23 73. *Thu-Tue 1200-1400 and 1930-2200.* Traditional Provençal rabbit or lamb *confit* is served up on the sunny, sheltered terrace. There's also a selection of salads, three set menus (from €25-34, including one that is 'bio', or all-organic) and a good wine list.

Manosque
€€€-€€ La Table du Pré Saint Michel, *Le Pré Saint Michel, route de Dauphin, Montée de la Mort d'Imbert*, T04 92 72 12 79. *Tue-Fri and Sun 1200-1400, Mon-Sat 1900-2200.* Tasty dishes, from goat's cheese and tomato tiramisu to chunky country-style pork terrine. Their three-course set menu (€26) also allows for a cheaper choice – two courses plus a glass of wine (€19). Chatty and charming staff really make this spot shine.

Valensole
€€€€-€€€ Hostellerie de la Fuste,
Lieu-dit La Fuste, T04 92 72 05 95, lafuste. com. *Tue-Sat 1200-1430 and 1900-2200, Sun 1200-1430.* Rustic Lubéron cooking from Chef Max François, who in 2011 took the helm from Daniel Jourdan, the restaurant's previous owner and resident chef since 1967. Ingredients are local, and most come straight from the chef's garden: rabbit terrine with juniper, violet artichokes with aged goat's cheese. More decadent patrons can splurge on the chef's selection of tasting dishes, Fuste's Menu Dégustation (€95).

◎ Shopping

Gordes *p59*
Souvenirs
La Méridienne, *Place du Château*, T04 90 72 06 99. *Daily 1000-1900.* Provençal bedspreads, ceramic salt and pepper shakers, sets of gardening tools and more.

Forcalquier
Food and drink
Distilleries et Domaines de Provence,
Av St-Promasse, T04 92 75 15 41, distilleries-
provence.com. Jul-Aug Mon-Sat 0900-1900,
Sun 0900-1300, Apr-Jun and Sep-Dec Mon
and Wed-Sat 1000-1230 and 1400-1900.
Sample award-winning (2011 silver medal
winner, International Wine and Spirit
Competition) Pastis Henri Bardouin at
the source.

Peyruis
Souvenirs
Lothantique, *7 espace St-Pierre, T04 92 68*
60 30, boutique-lothantique.com. Tue-Sat
0900-1700. Eco-friendly essential oils,
soaps and lotions, straight from Vogade
family producers.

◯ What to do

The Lubéron *p58*
Food and wine
Patricia Wells Cooking Classes, *Clos*
Chanteduc, Vaison-la-Romaine, patriciawells.
com. US$5000 per person. Week-long
lessons led by American-born Wells, guru of
French cuisine and author of the excellent
Bistro Cooking.
Reine Sammut Cooking School, *Auberge*
La Fenière, route de Lourmarin, Cadenet, T04
90 68 11 79, reinesammut.com. Thu or Fri
mornings, €145 per person. One of France's
finest female chefs, Reine offers three-hour
cooking lessons, followed by lunch.

Wellbeing
La Maison d'Ennea, *Hôtel Les Bories, route*
de l'Abbaye de Sénanque, Gordes, T04 90 72
00 51, hotellesbories.com. Essential oil-based
treatments, from anti-jetlag massage (€80)
to five-day 'regenerating' packages (€695).
L'Occitane, *Z.I. St-Maurice, Manosque,*
loccitane.com. Mon-Fri, closed 3rd week Aug
and 3rd week Dec. Contact the Manosque
Tourist Office (T04 92 72 16 00, accueil@

manosque-tourisme.com) to book a one-
hour free tour of L'Occitane's factory. Learn
how the natural bath products are made,
then shop at the on-site boutique.

⊖ Transport

It's easiest to explore the heart of Provence
using your own vehicle. Buses run between
most of the Lubéron's towns (see below).
Taxi Lubéron (T06 86 74 52 74, taxi-
luberon.com) operates in the region, and
can also arrange personalised tours.

Gordes *p59*
Two buses per day to Roussillon (20 mins,
Sun no buses), one to three buses per day
to Cavaillon (40 mins).

Roussillon *p60*
One to two buses per day to Gordes
(20 mins, Sun buses only during school
holidays), one to two buses per day to
Cavaillon (1 hr).

Bonnieux *p60*
One to four buses per day to Lacoste (20
mins), Ménerbes (30 mins) and Cavaillon
(1 hr).

Apt
Buses approximately every two hours to
Pont Julien (10 mins), Bonnieux (15 mins),
Cavaillon (1 hr) and Avignon (1hr 20).

ⓘ Directory

The Lubéron *p58*
Money Most Lubéron towns have an
ATM in the main square. It's best to travel
with some cash, as smaller shops and
restaurants often don't accept cards.
Medical services Centre Hospitalier
du Pays d'Apt, route de Marseille, BP
172, Apt T08 26 02 00 84. Pharmacy
on 3 rue Raspail, Bonnieux, T04 90 75
82 35; route d'Apt, Lourmarin, T04 90

68 20 25. **Post office** Place du Jeu de Boules, Gordes; avenue Victor Hugo, Apt; place de la Poste, Roussillon. **Tourist information** Le Château, Gordes, T04 90 72 02 75, gordes-village.com; 20 avenue Philippe de Girard, Apt, T04 90 74 03 18, ot-apt.fr; place de la Poste, Roussillon, T04 90 05 60 25, roussillon-provence. com; place H Barthelemy, Lourmarin, T04 90 68 10 77, lourmarin.com; 16 place du Docteur Joubert, Manosque, T04 92 72 16 00, manosque-tourisme.com. The **Couleur Pass Lubéron** (€5, valid for 1-4 persons, available from tourist offices throughout the Lubéron) gives discounts of up to 50% on 16 activities throughout the region, including the Ancienne Usine Mathieu, the Village des Bories and Montgolfière Vol-Terre.

Contents

Avignon, Arles & Western Provence

Avignon and around

Fleeing a troubled and turbulent Rome, Pope Clement V shifted Catholicism's power base to Avignon in 1309. While both he and his successor, Pope John XXII, were content to bed down in the town bishops' old Episcopal palace (now the Musée du Petit Palais), later leaders Pope Benedict XII and Pope Clement VI dedicated their time at the Church's helm to the construction of a palace worthy of the papacy: Avignon's huge Gothic Palais des Papes now acts as the city's main draw.

Impressive as the palace is, it's worth losing the crowds to explore this beautiful walled town further. Clamber up the Rocher des Doms, a tiered park with dazzling views over the River Rhône and the tiny town of Villeneuve-lez-Avignon's Fort St André. Or hop on the river's free shuttle boat and spend an afternoon on the verdant Ile de la Barthelasse.

Avignon → *For listings, see pages 73-77.*

Palais des Papes

ⓘ *Place du Palais des Papes, T04 90 27 50 00, palais-des-papes.com. Daily 1st 2 weeks Mar 0900-1830, mid Mar-Jun and mid Sep-Nov 0900-1900, Jul and 1st 2 weeks Sep 0900-2000, Aug 0900-2100, Nov-Feb 0930-1745 (ticket desks close 1 hr earlier). €10.50, €8.50 concessions, Palais and Pont €13, €10 concessions; under 8s free, free audioguide. Map: Avignon, p70.*

The Palais des Papes, or Popes' Palace, looms over Avignon's old town and is one of the largest Gothic buildings in Europe.

Visits begin in the Cour d'Honneur (Courtyard of Honour), before plunging into the Palais Vieux (Old Palace), designed by papal architect Pierre Poisson and built under the auspices of Pope Benedict XII. The informative audioguide will direct you through the Treasury, with recessed floors for stockpiling some of the Church's worldly goods, to the 46-m-high Pope's Tower and on through to the restored Grand Tinel Hall, which looks out over the palace gardens to the east. But it's only upon entering the Pope's Chamber (as painted vines clamber up the bright blue walls, the previous Spartan rooms are quickly forgotten) that you can begin to envision the pampered splendour to which these religious leaders were accustomed.

When Benedict XII died in 1342, Pope Clement VI and architect Jean de Louvres continued to expand his predecessor's monstrous project. The Chambre du Cerf (Stag's Room) marks your passage into the Palais Neuf (New Palace). Formerly the papal study, this room boasts floor-to-ceiling frescos: hunting and fishing scenes preserved for over 500 years under thick layers of paint, attributed to Italian artist Matteo Giovannetti.

Visitors are directed on through the north and south sacristies to the vast Great Chapel. Well worth the steep stairs are the panoramas over Villeneuve-lez-Avignon and the Rhône from atop the Palace; follow the signs for Le Café-Terrasse. The tour winds down with a wander through the Great Audience Hall, before passing through **La Bouteillerie** wine shop (tasting available from a couple of euros per glass) and out through the Palace's well-endowed gift shop.

Pont St-Bénézet

ⓘ *Rue Ferruce, entrance to left of Porte du Rhône, T04 90 27 51 16, palais-des-papes.com. Daily 1st 2 weeks Mar 0900-1830, mid Mar-mid Jun and mid Sep-Nov 0900-1900, Jul and 1st 2 weeks Sep 0900-2000, Aug 0900-2100, Feb-mid Mar 0930-1745 (ticket desks close 30 mins earlier). €4.50, €3.50 concessions, Palais des Papes and Pont €13, €10 concessions; under 8s free, free audioguide. Map: Avignon, p70.*

Poking halfway across the Rhône before dropping off abruptly, the Pont St-Bénézet (also called the Pont d'Avignon) is the city's public landmark, a neat contrast to the religious grandeur that is the Palais des Papes.

Not that its history is without mystique. During the 12th century, Bénézet, a shepherd from Ardèche, was ordered by God to go to Avignon and instruct the city's residents to build a bridge. After proving his divine worth by pitching an impossibly massive stone into the river, Bénézet was named a saint and the Pont St-Bénézet was constructed.

A vitally important connection between Lyon and the Mediterranean Sea, the bridge also served as an important crossing point for religious pilgrims en route to Spain. Rebuilt periodically due to frequent flooding, the bridge was eventually abandoned during the 17th century. It achieved widespread notoriety again during the 18th century, when composer Pierre Certon's 16th-century song *Sur le Pont d'Avignon* became a huge hit.

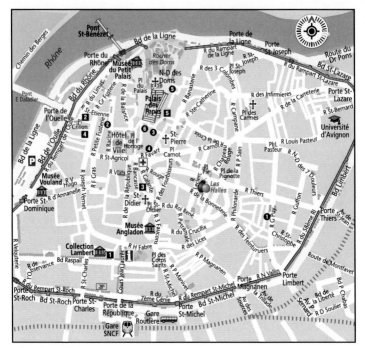

Where to stay

1 Hôtel Boquier
2 Hôtel d'Europe
3 Hôtel de Garlande
4 Hôtel Mignon
5 La Mirande

Restaurants

1 L'Atelier de Damien
2 La Fourchette
3 La Vache à Carreaux
4 Le Verso
5 Le Grand Café
6 Restaurant Christian Etienne

Musée du Petit Palais

ⓘ *Palais des Archevêques, place du Palais des Papes, T04 90 86 44 58, petit-palais.org. Wed-Mon 1000-1300 and 1400-1800. €6, €3 concessions, under 18s free, free Sun Sep-Jun. Map: Avignon, p70.*

Located in the former Archbishops' Palace, the Musée du Petit Palais houses collections of medieval and Renaissance works; Sandro Botticelli's *Madonna and Child* is the highlight of pieces on permanent display. The museum also stages temporary exhibitions.

Musée Angladon

ⓘ *5 rue Laboureur, T04 90 82 29 03, angladon.com. Tue-Sun 1300-1800, closed Tue in winter. €6, €4 concessions, €3 students, €1.50 child (7-12), under 7s free. Map: Avignon, p70.*

Owner of Parisian fashion house Doucet & Fils, Jacques Doucet assembled this small yet very personal collection of 17th- to 20th-century paintings, furniture and ceramics over the course of his lifetime. The artworks were eventually inherited by Doucet's grandnephew and his wife, Jean and Paulette Angladon-Dubrujeaud, and are now exhibited in their former home.

On the ground floor, standouts include Modigliani's *Portrait of a Woman*, Sisley's *Snow in Louveciennes*, Van Gogh's *Railroad Cars* and a bright green study for one of Degas' dancers. Upstairs, the collection ranges from French medieval to Tang sculptures. Temporary exhibitions (included in entrance fee) are often woven through the museum, such as the recent show of Robert Doisneau photos.

Musée Louis Vouland

ⓘ *17 rue Victor Hugo, T04 90 86 03 79, vouland.com. Tue-Sun Jul-Sep 1200-1800, Oct-Jun 1400-1800, closed Feb. €6, €4 concessions, under 12s free. Map: Avignon, p70.*

Louis Vouland's home from 1927 until his death in 1973, the Hôtel de Villeneuve-Esclapon now houses the industrial magnate's collection of primarily 18th century decorative arts. Although not large, the rooms themselves are cavernous; each one is dedicated to a different region or theme, from Vouland's luxuriant Chinese bedroom to cabinet displays of Marseillaise porcelain. Temporary exhibitions (included in the entrance fee) are playful and complementary: a recent highlight dotted antique and contemporary mirrors throughout.

Collection Lambert: Musée d'Art Contemporain

ⓘ *Hôtel de Caumont, 5 rue Violette, T04 90 16 56 20, collectionlambert.com. Jul-Aug 1100-1900, Sep-Jun Tue-Sun 1100-1800. €7, €5.50 concessions, €2 child (6-12), under 6s free. Map: Avignon, p70.*

Yvon Lambert opened this contemporary museum in 2000, providing Avignon with a much-needed counterbalance to the historical and religious art on permanent display. Each year, three exhibitions are showcased throughout the 18th-century Hôtel de Caumont's labyrinthine rooms. These range from spotlighting single artists, including New York photographer Roni Koon or Belgian video artist Francis Alÿs, to thematic exhibitions, such as post-20th century Japanese show, *Eijanaika, Yes Future!* The museum also houses a very good bookshop.

Around Avignon → *For listings, see pages 73-77.*

Sitting 18 and 29 km north of Avignon respectively, Châteauneuf-du-Pape and Orange are two of the region's most rewarding day trips. History buffs should head to the Théâtre Antique d'Orange, one of the best-preserved Roman theatres in existence today; wine aficionados will revel in Châteauneuf-du-Pape's first-class AOC vineyards. Note that getting around the area is difficult if you don't have your own transport.

Châteauneuf-du-Pape

Although the town's origins date to the 11th century, the area around Châteauneuf-du-Pape rose in importance during the 14th century, when the region was lavished with affection from Pope Clement V. The Avignon-based pope encouraged local wine production, and vineyards soon supplied the Papacy with year-round, top-notch *cru*. Pope John XXII took his passion a step further, overseeing the construction of Châteauneuf-du-Pape's **Château des Papes** and spending his summers there.

Today, most tourists visit the area for its sumptuous **vineyards**, see over page for a list of the best, which produce almost 14 million bottles of strong, Grenache noir, Syrah and Mourvèdre-based red AOC wines every year; just 6% of the AOC's annual production is white wine.

Try these vineyards in the Châteauneuf-du-Pape area:

Château Fortia ① *Route de Bédarrides, T04 90 83 72 25, chateau-fortia.com.*

Domaine Chante Cigale ① *Avenue Louis Pasteur, T04 90 83 70 57, chantecigale.com.*

Château Mont Redon ① *Route d'Orange, T04 90 83 72 75, chateaumontredon.fr.*

Vinadea Maison des Vins ① *8 rue Maréchal Foch, T04 90 83 70 69, vinadea.com.* Stocking wines from 90 nearby domaines.

Musée du Vin Père Anselme ① *Avenue Pierre de Luxembourg, T04 90 83 70 07, brotte.com; daily mid Apr-mid Oct 0900-1300 and 1400-1900, mid Oct-mid Apr 0900-1200 and 1400-1800; free.* Owned by the Brotte family since 1931, this wine museum represents four local domains: Le Château de Bord, Le Domaine Barville, Le Domaine Grosset and Le Domaine de l'Aube. Exhibits include a 14th-century chestnut wine barrel and a 16th-century wine press, plus on-site cellars.

Théâtre Antique d'Orange

① *Rue Madeleine Roch, T04 90 51 17 60, theatre-antique.com. Jun-Aug 0900-1900, Apr-May and Sep 0900-1800, May and Oct 0930-1730, Nov-Feb 0930-1630. €8.50, €6.50 concessions, under 7s free, free audioguide.*

Seating close to 10,000 spectators, the Théâtre Antique d'Orange was built under Emperor Augustus during the first century AD, with the theatre's tiered bench seating (*cavea*) fitted snugly into the Colline St-Eutrope hill; over the centuries, this mode of construction has helped to shelter the theatre as a whole. Its massive stage wall, 103 m x 37 m, remains uniquely intact, allowing visitors a clear picture of the theatre's towering dimensions. Near the complex entrance are the remains of a Roman temple.

During July, **Les Chorégies d'Orange** (choregies.asso.fr) opera festival takes place in the Théâtre Antique d'Orange; quirkier annual events are also staged here, including September's Roman Festival.

L'Isle-sur-la-Sorgue

① *Tourist information office: Place de la Liberté, T04 90 38 04 78, oti-delasorgue.fr, Mon-Sat 0900-1230 and 1430-1800, Jul-Aug Sun 0930-1300, Sep-Jun Sun 0900-1230. Frequent buses and trains run between L'Isle-sur-la-Sorgue, Avignon and Marseille. Buses stop on avenue des Quatres Otages, while the train station is just off avenue de l'Egalite; both are an easy walk from the town centre.*

Gushing forth at the pretty Provençal town of Fontaine de Vaucluse, the River Sorgue spills seven kilometres downstream to L'Isle-sur-la-Sorgue, a unique catchment of islands, waterways and picturesque bridges.

Originally a fishing village, during the Middle Ages the town morphed from a single island to a network of islets, as residents built canals, draining and firming the surrounding marshlands. L'Isle-sur-la-Sorgue gradually turned to larger-scale industry and giant waterwheels were installed on the canals. By the 19th century, an incredible 72 of these wheels served to power the local textile trade.

The very lucrative production of silk and wool paid off. Today, the town is still an affluent spot. Visit on a Sunday, when L'Isle-sur-la-Sorgue's **antique and brocante market** ① *from 0900, all day*, fills the streets. Over 300 stalls join the village's many (permanent) antique stores, drawing thousands of visitors from the surrounding countryside.

For a walking tour of the town, begin at the **Jardin Public** on the corner of avenue des Quatres Otages and allée 18 Juin 1940. (If you've taken the bus from Avignon, you'll hop off just over the road.) It's here you'll catch your first glimpse of one of L'Isle-sur-la-Sorgue's nine remaining **waterwheels**, slowly spinning and draped in deep green moss.

Head into the Old Town, crossing over one of the Sorgue's streams, which edges the southern half of the town, and quai Jean Jaurès. Walk through **place Rose Goudard**; on a Sunday, this square will be packed with olive oil soaps, Provençal bedspreads and stacks of salami. Continue along rue Rose Goudard, bending left toward the town's **Eglise Notre-Dame-des-Anges**. Constructed in 1222, the church was almost entirely rebuilt during the mid-17th century; its stunning Baroque interior also houses a resplendent organ.

Next door, the central tourist office is located in the town's former public granary, built in 1779. Poetry-lovers can dip down rue du Docteur Tallet to the **Campredon Centre d'Art** ① *Hôtel Donadeï de Campredon, 20 rue du Docteur Tallet, T04 90 38 17 41, islesurlasorgue.fr/campredon, Jul-Aug Tue-Sun 1000-1300 and 1500-1900, Sep-Jun Tue-Sun 1000-1230 and 1400-1730, €6, €5 students, under 14s free*. The museum has a permanent exhibition dedicated to the 20th-century poet René Char, who was born here, as well as contemporaneous temporary shows.

Alternatively, cross from the church to the opposite side of place de la Liberté, follow rue Danton to rue Jean Théophile and turn left. Half canal, half ambling alley, the street's left side is dotted with three waterwheels; wealthy old homes line the surrounding streets. Walk to rue Autheman, which marks the Old Town's former ramparts, and take another left. Look out for northbound rue Carnot, crowded with boutiques, bakeries and souvenir shops, while across place Char, avenue de l'Egalité is home to four large, permanent antique centres.

Continue straight along quai Rouget de Lisle to quai Jean Jaurès. Signposted on the left, antique shops selling 1920s posters, art deco garden furniture and old tin jugs cluster around La Cour, a small enclosed courtyard off the busy quay. Allée 18 Juin 1940 will take you back to your starting point near the public gardens.

To explore the River Sorgue and its crystal clear canals further, make your way along avenue des quatre Otages to avenue Charmasson. There's a **canoe and kayaking centre** ① *T04 90 38 33 22, canoe-sur-la-sorgue.com, mid Apr-mid Sep*, on the canal.

Avignon and around listings

For hotel and restaurant price codes and other relevant information, see pages 10-14.

🛏 Where to stay

Avignon *p69, map p70*
€€€€ La Mirande, *4 place de l'Amirande, T04 90 14 20 20, la-mirande.fr*. Stumble from the Palais des Papes over the road and into a palace of your own. Rooms are decked out with an eye for period detail: all sumptuous 18th-century, Provençal-inspired textiles and antiques. Foodies can book into one of Le Marmiton's (see page 76) on-site cooking lessons; a more sedate option is afternoon tea in the hotel garden.

€€€ Hôtel d'Europe, *12 place Crillon, T04 90 14 76 76, heurope.com*. With a roster of guests that reads like attendees of a wacky dinner party – Salvador Dali, Tennessee Williams, Charles Dickens and Napoleon, to name a few – it's surprising to find the Hôtel d'Europe so utterly unpretentious. Housed in a 16th-century mansion, 41 rooms and three spacious suites (the latter each with private balcony) cluster around a wisteria-draped courtyard.

€€€-€€ Hôtel de Garlande, *20 rue Galante, T04 90 80 08 85, hoteldegarlande. com*. Eleven simple rooms in a renovated city centre townhouse. With an unbeatable location just off place de l'Horloge, the Garlande is steps from a slew of lively bars and restaurants: light sleepers beware. A/C and free Wi-Fi; no lift.

€€ Hôtel Mignon, *12 rue Joseph-Vernet, T04 90 82 17 30, hotel-mignon.com.* Wedged in among rue Joseph-Vernet's back-to-back boutiques, Hôtel Mignon's 16 petite bedrooms couldn't be further from the neighbourhood's edgy trends. Simple bright walls complement Provençal-printed fabrics, as do exposed beams in some of the rooms. Unusually for these parts, breakfast is included (mid and high seasons only), and there's a computer (free internet access for guests) in the foyer.

€€-€ Hôtel Boquier, *6 rue du Portail Boquier, T04 90 82 34 43, hotel-boquier.com.* This welcoming spot may be the city's best budget find: 12 airy rooms located just inside the Porte de la République. Friendly owners Sylvie and Pascal have renovated the 18th-century building, and many of the bedrooms now sport unfussy themed furnishings (eg. Moroccan, Indian or Lavender). Book well in advance.

Châteauneuf-du-Pape *p71*

€€€€-€€€ Hostellerie du Château des Fines Roches, *Route de Sorgues, T04 90 83 70 23, chateaufinesroches.com. Closed Sun-Mon Nov-Apr.* A 19th-century castle set among rambling vineyards and Tuscan cypress. Previously owned by the Marquis Falco de Baroncelli-Javon, the castle's 11 elegant rooms (rolltop bathtubs, canopied beds) have views over the Château des Papes and Mont Ventoux. There's also an outdoor pool and restaurant with panoramic terrace.

€€ The Wine B&B, *Bastide Chante Alouette, 20 av Général de Gaulle, T04 90 83 79 38, chateauneuf-wine-bb.com. Oct-Apr open by advance reservation only.* Owned by expert sommelier Danièle Raulet-Reynaud, this cute B&B is located in the heart of Châteauneuf village. Three charming rooms, plus a 'cosy corner' common room, stocked with books on local wines, and a central garden, where breakfast is served during the summer.

L'Isle-sur-la-Sorgue *p72*

€€€€ La Maison sur la Sorgue, *6 rue Rose Goudard, T06 87 32 58 68, lamaisonsurlasorgue.com.* Four unique rooms as pampering as they are personal. La Maison is owned by Marie-Claude, a L'Isle native brimming with undiscovered local tips, and the gregarious Frédéric, who mans their objets d'art-cum-furnishings shop, Retour de Voyage, next door. An ideal base, far from the region's tourist crowds; breakfast (included) is locally sourced.

🍴 Restaurants

Avignon *p69, map p70*

€€€€-€€€ Restaurant Christian Etienne, *10 rue de Mons, T04 90 86 16 50, christian-etienne.fr. Tue-Sat 1200-1315 and 1930-2115, closed 2 weeks Nov.* With a terrace overlooking the Palais des Papes, this Michelin-starred restaurant is easily the chicest spot in town. Go for Etienne's summertime special, the €65 Menu Tomate, featuring heirloom tomato sorbet; gourmets on a budget can opt for the three-course €31 lunch menu instead.

€€€-€€ La Fourchette, *17 rue Racine, T04 90 85 20 93. Mon-Fri 1215-1345 and 1915-2145.* Informal, cosy and stylish, La Fourchette's walls are adorned with quirky cutlery. In the evening, the three-course menu (€33) may include saffron salmon with leek fondue, or *daube Avignonnaise*. During summer months, the bay windows are removed, making both dining rooms open and airy.

€€€-€€ La Vache à Carreau, *14 rue de la Peyrollerie, T04 90 80 09 05. Sun 1230-1430 and 1930-2230, Sat 1930-2330.* A cheese-lover's paradise, dishing up everything from salmon with goat's cheese to hot Camembert steeped in garlic. Dip into their cellar for local wines to match. Exposed stone walls, low lighting and excellent jazz make for a fun and romantic ambience.

€€-€ L'Atelier de Damien, *54 rue Guillaume Puy, T04 90 82 57 35. Tue-Sat 1200-1400 and 1930-2130.* Damien Demazure, who trained in the kitchens of Cannes' Michelin-starred La Palme d'Or, opened this petite restaurant in 2010, far off of Avignon's all-too-trodden tourist trail. It's well worth seeking out. Lunchtime *plats du jour* are a bargain €9.50 (such as salmon rôti with mashed potatoes); at dinner, Damien's three-course menu is just €26.

€€-€ Le Verso, *3 place Nicolas Saboly, T04 90 85 28 89. Daily 1200-1400, 1930-2230.* The place to go for Avignon's finest, real Italian pizzas: thin, crispy and generously laden with toppings; wines by the *pichet*.

Cafés and bars
Le Grand Café, *4 rue des Escaliers Ste-Anne, T04 90 86 86 77, legrandcafe-avignon.fr. Tue-Sat 1200-1430 and 1900-2300.* Artsy café and bar in a pretty courtyard, next door to **Cinéma Utopia** (see right).

Châteauneuf-du-Pape *p71*
€€€-€€ La Mère Germaine, *3 rue du Commandant Lemaitre, T04 90 22 78 34, lameregermaine.fr. Daily 1200-1400, Mon-Sat 1930-2130.* A tasty, traditional restaurant and wine bar, opened by Parisian chef Germaine Vion in 1922. The legendary restaurant was fully renovated and reopened in 2011 by new owner André Mazy; chef Eric Balan is now at the kitchen's helm. Set menus from €14-23; the Châteauneuf-stocked wine cellar is superb.

Orange *p72*
€€€-€ Le Parvis, *55 cours Pourtoules, T04 90 34 82 00. Tue-Sun 1230-1400, Tue-Sat 1900-2230.* Chef Jean-Michel Bérengier serves up outstanding value *plats du jour* (from €10 apiece) on a terrace just around the corner from the Théâtre Antique. His pricier evening menus (€28-48) may

include aubergine marmalade paired with tomato *coulis*, or red mullet and shitake mushrooms in a sesame crust.

L'Isle-sur-la-Sorgue *p72*
€€€€-€€ La Prévôté, *4 rue Jean-Jacques Rousseau, T04 90 38 57 29, la-prevote.fr. Thu-Mon 1230-1400, 1930-2130, closed Wed Sep-Jun.* In a former church sacristy, Jean-Marie Alloin's three-course lunch menu (€28, except Sun) gives you free rein over the seasonal menu, and includes two glasses of wine. Opt for courgette flowers with summer truffles, or the fig and rhubarb tart.

€€-€ L'Islot Vert, *52/54 rue Carnot, T04 90 24 86 62, islotvert.com. Tue-Fri 1200-1415, Fri-Sat 1930-2130.* All-organic spot in downtown L'Isle: go for the Fraicheur plate (€12.50), which features seasonal local ingredients, or grab a 'bio'wich' (organic sandwich, €8.50, price includes a glass of freshly-squeezed juice) to take away.

Entertainment

Avignon *p69, map p70*
Cinema
Cinéma Utopia, *4 rue des Escaliers Ste-Anne, Avignon, T04 90 82 65 36, cinemas-utopia. org/avignon.* Original language films, shown daily. Additional screening room at 5 rue Figuière.

Clubs
Le Privé, *Lieu-dit Les Cavernes, Route de Tavel, Les Angles, Avignon, T06 17 76 42 14, leprive.tv. Tue 2100-0600, Wed-Sat 2400-0600.* Historic mostly techno club in a former quarry, just outside the city.

Shopping

Avignon *p69, map p70*
Shakespeare, *155 rue de la Carreterie, Avignon, T04 90 27 38 50. Tue-Sat 0930-1200 and 1400-1800.* English-language books and DVDs, plus tearoom serving English cream tea with homemade scones.

⚙ What to do

Avignon and around *p69, map p70*
Canoeing and kayaking
Kayak Vert, *Fontaine de Vaucluse, T04 90 20 35 44, canoefrance.com. Daily Mar-Oct, €34 canoe (max 2 adults and 1 child under 8), €17 kayak (1 adult), students €14, prices include return to Fontaine de Vaucluse by bus.* Canoe or kayak from Fontaine de Vaucluse 8 km down the River Sorgue to L'Isle-sur-la-Sorgue.

Bicycle hire
Giuliani Location Vélo, *40 chemin St-Etienne, Bédarrides, T04 90 33 10 30, location-velo-vaucluse.com. From €17/day; free delivery to your hotel.* Cycle through the vineyards that surround Châteauneuf-du-Pape.

Cultural
Avignon City Tours, *Office de Tourisme, 41 cours Jean Jaurès, Avignon, T04 32 74 32 74, avignon-tourisme.com.* Historical walking tours of Avignon's city centre. 'When the Popes lived in Avignon': April-June and August-October Monday 1030, departing from the Palais des Papes ticket office, €19, under 8s free; 'The Secret Palais des Papes': September-May Friday 1500, €24, adults only.

Food and wine
Laboratoire d'œnologie Mouriesse, *2 rue des Papes, Châteauneuf-du-Pape, T04 90 83 56 15, oenologie-mouriesse.com.* Wine-tasting school. Courses range from introductory (2 hrs, €40 per person) to professional (price varies).
La Mirande and Le Marmiton Cooking School, *4 place de l'Amirande, Avignon, T04 90 14 20 20, la-mirande.fr. Closed Jul and Aug, from €80.* Twice a week chef Jean-Claude Altmayer puts together a historically accurate meal in the hotel's 19th-century kitchen (Tue-Wed 2000, max 14 guests, €86 per person including

wine; it's also possible to cook the meal alongside Chef Altmayer, Tue-Wed 1800, €160 per person). Bilingual cooking classes also on site; instructors include Christian Etienne and Bruno d'Angelis, chef at the Hôtel d'Europe.
Provence Panorama, *37 av Pierre Sémard, Avignon, T04 90 29 76 05, provencetours-avignon.com.* Half-day vineyard tours to Châteauneuf-du-Pape and around. From €55 per person, including hotel pick-up.

⊖ Transport

Avignon *p69, map p70*
Avignon's Old Town is small and best navigated on foot. A shuttle bus (tcra.fr, 10 mins, departures every 20 mins) runs between the TGV station and Porte de la République. There's a taxi stand at Porte de la République, or you can arrange a pick-up on T04 90 82 20 20.

Avignon's bike-sharing scheme has put 200 sturdy bikes on to the city streets. Buy a day (€1) or week (€5) pass at one of the 18 stations dotted around town; bike use is free for up to 30 minutes a pop. More info can be found at velopop.fr.

Train stations: Gare TGV Quartier de Courtine; Gare SNCF, boulevard St Roch. Frequent trains to Arles (20-25 mins) and on to Marseille (1hr 10). Bus station: 5 avenue Monclar, T04 90 82 07 35. One to three buses daily to Châteauneuf-du-Pape (45 mins-1 hr; no buses Sun). Four to eight buses daily to St-Rémy (45 mins).

Châteauneuf-du-Pape *p71*
One to two buses daily to Avignon (45 mins-1 hr; no buses Sun).

Orange *p72*
From Avignon, Orange is 12 minutes by train or 45 minutes by bus. Train station: Avenue Frédéric Mistral, Orange, T04 90 11 88 03. Bus station: Parking de l'Arc de Triomphe, Orange, T04 90 34 15 59.

L'Isle-sur-la-Sorgue *p72*
Seven to 12 daily trains to Avignon (25
mins); 5-8 daily trains to Marseille (1hr 20).

❶ Directory

Avignon *p69, map p70*
Money Plenty of ATMs throughout the
town, including along cours Jean Jaurès.
Medical services Hôpital Général Henri
Duffaut, 305 rue Raoul Follereau, T04 32
75 33 33, ch-avignon.fr. **Pharmacie Tarot**,
29 rue Marchands, T04 90 82 27 91. **Post
office** Cours Président Kennedy, T36
31 (Mon-Fri 0830-1830, Sat 0830-1200).
Tourist information 41 cours Jean Jaurès,
T04 32 74 32 74, avignon-tourisme.com
(Apr-Oct Mon-Sat 0900-1800 and Sun
0945-1700, during Jul daily 0900-1900, Nov-
Mar Mon-Fri 0900-1800, Sat 0900-1700, Sun
1000-1200). Available at the tourist office,
major sights and most hotels, the **Avignon
Passion card** offers discounted visits to the
city's cultural highlights. Pay full entrance
to any monument or museum, making
sure your pass is stamped. You and up
to four other people will then be entitled
to 10-50% off regular entry fees at other
sights. The pass is valid for 15 days.

Around Avignon *p71*
Money Plenty of ATMs in Orange,
including two on rue de la République.

It's best to have cash to hand if you're
heading into the surrounding countryside.
Medical services Centre Hospitalier
Louis Giorgi, avenue de Lavoisier, Orange,
T04 90 11 22 22. **Pharmacie Arausio**, 4 rue
St Martin, Orange, T04 90 34 10 64. **Post
office** 679 boulevard Edouard Daladier,
Orange, T36 34 (Mon-Fri 0830-1215
and 1330-1800, Saturday 0830-1200).
Tourist information Offices at: 5 cours
Aristide Briand, Orange, T04 90 34 70 88,
uk.otorange.fr (Jul-Aug Mon-Sat 0900-
1930, Sun and holidays 1000-1300 and
1400-1830, Apr-Jun and Sep Mon-Sat
0900-1830, Sun and holidays 1000-1300
and 1400-1830, Oct-Mar Mon-Sat 1000-
1300 and 1400-1700) and place du Portail,
Châteauneuf-du-Pape, T04 90 83 71 08,
pays-provence.fr (Jun-Sep Mon-Sat 0930-
1800, Oct-May Mon-Tue and Thu-Sat 0930-
1230 and 1400-1800). The Châteauneuf-
du-Pape office produces various handouts
charting hikes and cycling routes around
the region. Two of the best are the bilingual
'From the vineyards of Châteauneuf-du-
Pape to the Ouvèze plain', a 28.5-km bike
trail that takes in Sorgues and Bédarrides,
and 'A la découverte de Châteauneuf-du-
Pape' (French only), a 1½-hour walk around
Châteauneuf-du-Pape's Old Town. These
itineraries, plus various others, can be
downloaded from ccpro.fr.

Les Baux and St-Rémy

Nestled within Les Alpilles mountain range south of Avignon, the towns of Les Baux-de-Provence and St-Rémy-de-Provence are postcard perfect, each in their own distinct way.

Les Baux-de-Provence → *For listings, see pages 80-81.*

Les Baux, a fortified village built of pale, golden stone, is laced with winding, medieval streets and skirted with heart-stopping vistas. Synonymous with Les Baux are the sprawling ruins of the **Château des Baux**, perched on the highest rocky tip of the town, overlooking olive groves and vineyards all the way to the sea. Within the village, the **Yves Brayer Museum** ⓘ *T04 90 54 36 99, yvesbrayer.com, Apr-Sep daily 1000-1230 and 1400-1830, Oct-Mar Wed-Mon 1000-1230 and 1400-1700, closed Jan-mid Feb, €5, under 18s free*, dedicated to the 20th-century painter, and the **Musée des Santons** ⓘ *T04 90 54 34 39, free*, a display of nativity scene figurines ranging from 17th century Neapolitan to 19th century papier-mâché, both have unusual collections.

Château des Baux

ⓘ *T04 90 54 55 56, chateau-baux-provence.com. Summer 0900-2030, autumn 0930-1800, winter 1000-1700, spring 0900-1950. Apr-Sep €9, €7 concessions; Oct-Mar €8, €6 concessions; under 7s free, free audioguide.*

Les Baux's unique position, seemingly balanced atop an Alpilles mountain peak, makes the town an ideal military vantage point. Château des Baux, built during the 10th century by the Lords of Les Baux, was coveted from the moment it was constructed. During the 15th century, the castle was taken over by the Masons des Comtes de Provence barons. Successive French kings later spent 200 years battling for its control, before ownership passed to Monaco's Grimaldis in 1643. The 7-ha Château and surrounding walled village eventually fell into disrepair, until its revival as a tourist attraction during the 20th century.

And what an attraction it is. From Easter until early autumn, expect to join hundreds of visitors exploring the Château, dungeon, Saracen and Paravelle towers, as well as the giant replica catapults and medieval siege weapons. The site also includes vestiges of daily life over the centuries, including townhouses, the Chapelle St-Blaise and a squat windmill. Walk out to the precipitous edge of the Château's southern plateau to admire breathtaking panoramas (all the way to the Camargue on a clear day). Note that during cooler weather, the *mistral* gusts across this area in particular.

Carrières de Lumières

ⓘ *Route de Maillane, T04 90 54 55 56, carrieres-lumieres.com. Daily Apr-Sep 1000-1900, Oct-Mar 1000-1800 (ticket desks close 1 hr earlier). €8.50, €6.50 child (7-17), Carrières de Lumières and Château Apr-Sep €14.50, €11 students/child (7-17), Oct-Mar €13.50, €10 students/child (7-17), under 7s free.*

Just outside Les Baux in the Val d'Enfer (Hell Valley), the Carrières de Lumières is located within former quarries. It was here in 1959 that Jean Cocteau filmed his *Testament d'Orphée*, with Picasso's participation. The space was completely renovated in 2011, and today it is used for annual exhibitions: the stone walls, ceilings and columns serve as natural screens on to which images of artworks are projected. An impressive Gauguin and Van Gogh exhibition was the venue's 2012 highlight.

St-Rémy-de-Provence → For listings, see pages 80-81.

In contrast to Les Baux, St-Rémy is peppered with second homes, a wealthy bolthole overflowing with affluent French city-dwellers come the weekend. Head into its alluring Old Town and it's easy to see the appeal. St-Rémy was **Nostradamus's birthplace**: the signposted home (rue Hoche) is tucked down a tiny alley amongst the town's chicer shops. **Van Gogh** also lived here for an artistically prolific year, albeit at the psychiatric hospital of the **Monastère St-Paul de Mausole** just south of town.

Musée Estrine
ⓘ *8 rue Estrine, T04 90 92 34 72. May-Sep Thu-Mon 1000-1230 and 1400-1900, Wed 1000-1800, mid Mar-Apr and Oct-Nov Wed-Mon 1030-1230 and 1400-1800. €3.20, St-Rémy Pass €2.30, €1.30 students, under 12s free.*
Located within an 18th-century mansion, the Musée Estrine houses the *Centre d'Interprétation Van Gogh*, a permanent exhibition space that includes replicas of the artist's paintings, plus photos, letters and an annual selection of projected images. Also within the museum, 20 artworks by 20th-century cubist Albert Gleizes, who resided in St-Rémy from 1939 until his death in 1952, are displayed over two rooms. There are occasional temporary shows on site as well. Note that the museum will be closed from April 2012 until summer 2013 for renovations.

Monastère St-Paul de Mausole
ⓘ *Chemin de St-Paul, T04 90 92 77 00, cloitresaintpaul-valetudo.com. Daily Apr-Sep 0930-1900, Oct-Mar 1015-1645, closed Jan. €4, St-Rémy Pass €3, under 12s free.*
A psychiatric centre since the 15th century, this monastery continues to serve as a retreat, providing therapy for the mentally ill. Its most famous patient was Van Gogh, who lived here from 1889-1890, creating 143 paintings (including his famous *Starry Night*) and over 100 drawings during this brief but artistically intense period.

Visitors can take in the monastery's chapel, 11th- and 12th-century cloisters, the peaceful gardens and a re-creation of Van Gogh's bedroom. There's also a permanent exhibition of artworks for sale, created by current patients.

Site Archéologique de Glanum
ⓘ *Route des Baux-de-Provence, T04 90 92 23 79, glanum.monuments-nationaux.fr. Apr-Sep daily 0930-1830 (closed Mon in Sep), Oct-Mar Tue-Sun 1000-1700. €7.50, St-Rémy Pass €5.50, €4.50 18-25s, under 18s/EU citizens under 26 free.*
Just around the corner from the Monastère St-Paul lie the ruins of Glanum, first a Celto-Ligurian, then Gallo-Greek and later Gallo-Roman, city. Excavations, which began in 1921, date finds from the sixth century BC to the third century AD, when the city was abandoned. The superb site's highlights include the sacred spring area, Roman temples and baths.

Over the route des Baux (also called avenue Vincent Van Gogh), **Les Antiques** – a well-preserved triumphal arch and mausoleum – have been attracting visitors since the 16th century.

Les Baux and St-Rémy listings

For hotel and restaurant price codes and other relevant information, see pages 10-14.

◉ Where to stay

Les Baux-de-Provence *p78*
€€-€ Hostellerie de la Reine Jeanne, *Rue Porte Mage, T04 90 54 32 06, la-reinejeanne. com.* Nine bargain doubles and one apartment for four (€100), in business since 1905 and just inside Les Baux's walled village. The terrace overlooks the valley below; the excellent on-site restaurant offers half-board options.

St-Rémy-de-Provence *p79*
€€€€-€€€ Hôtel les Ateliers de l'Image, *36 bd Victor Hugo, T04 90 92 51 50, hoteldelimage.com. Closed Nov-early Mar.* A verdant oasis on the edge of St-Rémy's old town, with 27 rooms and five suites (including the charming Tree House Suite) spread over two wings – the Espace Atelier, previously a cinema and music hall, and the Espace Provence, the former Hôtel de Provence. There's a swimming pool, a restaurant and a cocktail bar on site.
€€€€-€€€ La Maison du Village, *10 rue du 8 Mai 1945, T04 32 60 68 20, lamaisonduvillage.com.* In an 18th-century townhouse, subtle Provençal hues deck the walls and decor of five sumptuous boudoirs. Downstairs, common areas are comprised of two drawing rooms and a dining room, a Diptyque sales corner (Parisian perfumes, bath products and candles) in the reception area and a walled garden with antique fountain out back. Ideal for a romantic weekend *à deux*.
€€-€ Le Sommeil des Fées, *4 rue du 8 Mai 1945, T04 90 92 17 66, T04 90 92 17 66, angesetfees-stremy.com.* Five simple, friendly B&B rooms in the heart of St-Rémy; the abundant breakfast includes homemade bread, croissants and plenty of local fruit jams. On the ground floor,

courtyard restaurant La Cuisine des Anges serves up simple Provençal fare.

❼ Restaurants

Les Baux-de-Provence *p78*
€€ Café des Baux, *Rue Trencat, T04 90 54 52 69. Jul-Aug 1200-1500 and 1900-2130, Apr-Jun and Sep-Oct 1200-1500.* Perched at the top of the village, Café des Baux boasts a sunny, sheltered courtyard, much appreciated after exploring the exposed Château. Big seasonal salads are named after artists (the Picasso, or the Matisse), while divine desserts – try the caramel *pavé* with chocolate biscuits – are created by specialist chef Pierre Walter.

St-Rémy-de-Provence *p79*
€€€-€€ L'Aile ou la Cuisse, *5 rue de la Commune, T04 32 62 00 25. Tue-Sat boutique traiteur 1000-1900, restaurant Tue-Sat 1200-1430, 1930-2200.* Combination upscale deli and country cooking. At lunchtime, pick up a quick picnic; or book an evening table on the patio and order their signature dish *l'aile et la cuisse de coquelet* (cockerel wing and thigh), served with creamy morel mushrooms (€28).
€€€-€€ Mistral Gourmand, *12 av Durand Maillane, T04 90 92 14 65. Jun-Aug Mon-Sat 1200-1430 and 1930-2200, Sep-May Tue-Sat 1200-1430 and 1930-2200.* Catering for locals rather than tourists in transit, this easy-to-miss restaurant dishes up exceptional Provençal cuisine. Try chanterelle mushrooms with *lardons* and egg, or the shrimp 'bouquet' served with homemade *aïoli*. The top wine list has also been selected with care.

◉ Shopping

St-Rémy-de-Provence *p79*
Joël Durand, *3 bd Victor Hugo, St-Rémy-de-Provence, T04 90 92 38 25, chocolat-durand.*

com. Mon-Sat 0930-1230 and 1430-1930 (Mon until 1900), Sun and hols 1000-1300 and 1430-1900. Heavenly chocolates, caramels and candied fruits from one of France's premier *chocolatiers*.

Moulin à Huile du Calanquet, *Vieux chemin d'Arles, St-Rémy-de-Provence, T04 32 60 09 50, moulinducalanquet.fr. Mon-Sat 0900-1200 and 1400-1830, Sun 1000-1200 and 1500-1800.* Traditional olive oil mill, plus boutique selling Alpilles olive oil, olives, tapenade, jams and chutneys.

What to do

St-Rémy-de-Provence *p79*
Classic Bike Esprit, *17a av de la Première DFL, St-Rémy-de-Provence, T04 90 26 03 19, jebike.com.* Classic motorcycles and sidecars to rent, from €125/day.

Transport

Both the Les Baux and St-Rémy Old Towns can only be explored on foot. During high season, buses run between the two towns, though you'll need your own transport or a taxi to reach Les Baux if you're travelling from October to May. In St-Rémy, try **Taxi Leinez** (T04 90 92 86 73), in Les Baux **Taxi Delepierre** (T06 80 27 60 92) or book through the tourist office.

Les Baux-de-Provence *p78*
Four buses daily (Jul-Aug only), Saturday-Sunday and hols only June and September to St-Rémy (15 mins; no buses Oct-May).

St-Rémy-de-Provence *p79*
Four to eight buses daily to Avignon (45 mins). Four buses daily (Jul-Aug only), Saturday-Sunday and hols only June and September to Les Baux and Arles (15 mins and 50 mins; no buses Oct-May). Buses stop at place de la République, on the avenue Durand Maillane corner.

Directory

Les Baux and St-Rémy *p78*
Money Plenty of ATMs in St-Rémy, including on cours Mirabeau and boulevard Victor Hugo. **Medical services** Pharmacies on **Maussane les Alpilles**, Les Baux, T04 90 54 30 40; **Cendre**, cours Mirabeau, St-Rémy, T04 90 92 08 05. **Post office** Rue Roger Salengro, St-Rémy, T36 31. **Tourist information** Maison du Roy, Les Baux, T04 90 54 34 39, lesbauxdeprovence.com (Sat-Sun and holidays 1000-1730, May-Sep Mon-Fri 0900-1800, Oct-Apr Mon-Fri 0930-1700); place Jean Jaurès, St-Rémy, T04 90 92 05 22, saintremy-de-provence.com (Jul-Aug Mon-Sat 0900-1230 and 1400-1900, Sun 1000-1230 and 1400-1700, Apr-Jun and Sep-Oct 0900-1230 and 1400-1830, Sun 1000-1230, Oct-Apr Mon-Sat 0900-1230 and 1400-1730). Available at the tourist office and major sights, the **St-Rémy Pass** offers discounts on visits to the Musée Estrine, Musée des Alpilles, Monastère St-Paul de Mausole and Site Archéologique de Glanum. Pay full price for your first site's entrance and get your pass stamped. You'll then receive around 30% off additional entry fees. The pass is valid for 15 days.

Arles

Capital of the Camargue, home to an impressive amphitheatre and the short-term residence for one of the world's most famous painters, the petite Provençal city of Arles has attractions to please any visitor. Aspiring artists will appreciate a wander through place du Forum, where Café Van Gogh still looks pretty similar to its portrayal in the artist's painting, *Terrasse du Café le Soir,* while in late 2012, the Fondation Van Gogh will open their brand-new headquarters in the city's historical hôtel particulier Léautaud de Donines. Amateur archaeologists can delve into ruins that range from Roman baths to Gothic cloisters. And nature-lovers (particularly bird spotters) would do well to use the riverside city as a base, making daytime forays into the Parc Naturel Régional de Camargue to its south.

Amphithéâtre

ⓘ *Rond-point des Arènes, T04 90 49 59 05, arenes-arles.com. Daily May-Sep 0900-1900 (Wed Jul-Aug until 1500), Mar-Apr and Oct 0900-1800, Nov-Feb 1000-1700, ticket desk closes 30 mins earlier. €6.50, €5 students, under 18s free, ticket also allows entry to the Théâtre Antique.*
Built towards the end of the first century AD, Arles's amphitheatre was inspired by Rome's Coliseum, constructed around a decade earlier. Like the Roman theatre, large arches (two levels, 30 per level) ring the outer wall. Audiences of 20,000, seated along 34 tiers of internal benching, poured into the amphitheatre to watch re-enactments of famous battles, gladiators and humans pitted against beasts.

By the Middle Ages, the amphitheatre had slowly morphed into an actual town, as residents built hundreds of homes, businesses and two churches within the fortified walls. However the 1820s saw the structure cleared out; in 1830, the city held its first bullfight here, celebrating the French army's occupation of Algiers.

Today, visitors can wander the galleries and *cavea*, scaling the amphitheatre for towering views over the Old Town and the River Rhône. During July and August, Camargue **bull races** ⓘ *Wed 1700, €9, €4 child (6-12), under 6s free*, and **gladiator combat shows** ⓘ *Tue and Thu 1600-1830, free with entrance ticket*, are staged in the amphitheatre.

Théâtre Antique

ⓘ *Rue de la Calade, T04 90 49 59 05. Daily May-Sep 0900-1900, Mar-Apr and Oct 0900-1800, Nov-Feb 1000-1700, ticket desk closes 30mins earlier. €6.50, €5 students, under 18s free, ticket also allows entry to the Amphithéâtre.*
Just south of the city's Amphithéâtre, the ruins of Arles's first-century BC Théâtre Antique are tucked into a residential Old Town neighbourhood. It was here, in 1651, that the stunning two-metre *Venus* sculpture (also dating from the first century BC, and now in the Louvre) was discovered while labourers were digging a well.

Seating 10,000 spectators in its heyday, the theatre now hosts various performances throughout the summer, including **Les Suds** (suds-arles.com) and the **Fête du Costume** (festivarles.com, both July).

Cloître St-Trophime

ⓘ *Place de la République, T04 90 49 59 05. Daily May-Sep 0900-1900, Mar-Apr and Oct 0900-1800, Nov-Feb 1000-1700, ticket desk closes 30 mins earlier. €3.50, €2.60 students, under 18s free.*
The St-Trophime cloisters were constructed in two distinct periods between the 12th and 14th centuries, resulting in a mix of Romanesque and Gothic architecture. Carved columns surround a central courtyard; the complex also includes a refectory, dormitory and the bishop's palace. Rooms surrounding the cloisters are often used to host contemporary art and photo exhibitions. Next door, the façade of **Cathédrale St-Trophime** sports an intricate, disturbing carved depiction of St John's Last Judgment.

Espace Van Gogh

ⓘ *Place Docteur Félix Rey, T04 90 49 39 39, mediatheque.ville-arles.fr. Free access to courtyard.*
Formerly Hôtel-Dieu, the hospital where Van Gogh was admitted after taking a razor to his ear, Espace Van Gogh is a now a cheery cultural centre. A *médiathèque*, temporary exhibition halls and a gift shop surround the bright plant-filled courtyard. The central gardens have been recreated to emulate the flowerbeds as they appeared during Van Gogh's stay.

Thermes de Constantin

ⓘ *Rue Dominique Maisto, T04 90 49 59 05. Daily May-Sep 0900-1200 and 1400-1900, Mar-Apr and Oct 0900-1200 and 1400-1800, Nov-Feb 1000-1200 and 1400-1700, ticket desk closes 30 mins earlier. €3, €2.20 students, under 18s free.*

Just a fraction of their sprawling fourth-century size, Arles's Roman baths were constructed under Emperor Constantine I. The public baths still contain portions of the original frigidarium, tepidarium and caldarium, the latter heated by roaring fires, funnelling hot air through brick piping in the walls. There's a unique rounded vault built of layers of limestone interspersed with brick, as well as the remains of a heated pool and a gymnasium.

Musée Réattu

ⓘ *10 rue du Grand Prieuré, T04 90 49 37 58, museereattu.arles.fr. Tue-Sun Jul-Sep 1000-1900, Oct-Jun 1000-1230 and 1400-1830, due to be closed for renovations until Jun 2010. €7, €5 students, under 18s free, free 1st Sun of month.*

This small but densely packed museum is a delightful contrast to the city's largely ancient monuments. Modern and contemporary artworks are hung throughout the 15th-century building, formerly the Grand Priory of the Knights of Malta. Picasso is well represented, as are early 20th-century photographers, including Edward Weston.

South of Old Town

As well as the city's downtown historical highlights, it's worth venturing south of boulevard des Lices to explore a few other exceptional sites. **Les Alyscamps** ⓘ *av des Alyscamps, daily May-Sep 0900-1900, Mar-Apr and Oct 0900-1200 and 1400-1800, Nov-Feb 1000-1200 and 1400-1700, €3.50, €2.60 students, under 18s free*, is a Roman necropolis; both Van Gogh and Paul Gauguin painted the burial ground here in 1888.

On the banks of the Rhône, the **Musée d'Arles Antique** ⓘ *Museum of Ancient Arles, presqu'île du Cirque Romain, T04 13 31 51 03, arles-antique.cg13.fr, Wed-Mon 1000-1800, €6, €4.50 students, under 18s free*, comprehensively covers Arles's history from prehistoric times through to the sixth century AD. The remains of a **Roman racetrack** are partially unearthed outside.

A pleasant half-hour's stroll south along the Canal d'Arles will bring you to Pont de Langlois, better known as Van Gogh's bridge. While not quite identical to the artist's *Le Pont de Langlois* (the bridge was originally positioned a few kilometres downstream), the current setting mirrors the 1888 painting.

Arles listings

For hotel and restaurant price codes and other relevant information, see pages 10-14.

🍽 Where to stay

Arles *p82*
€€€€-€€€ Grand Hôtel Nord Pinus, *Place du Forum, T04 90 93 44 44, nord-pinus. com*. The city's top historical hotel – both a favourite with visiting bullfighters (the designated room remains), as well as artists and authors, Picasso and Hemingway included. Decor in the bar and lounge evokes the hotel's 1950s heyday. Well-positioned for visiting the city's central sights.

€€€ Hôtel du Forum, *10 place du Forum, T04 90 93 48 95, hotelduforum.com*.

Closed Nov-Mar. Across from the buzzing square with Van Gogh's famed café, Hôtel du Forum boasts an outdoor pool (an essential delight during Arles's sweltering summers), stylish bar with billiard table and free Wi-Fi. Rooms are a little dated, but pleasantly quirky.

€€€ Le Calendal, *5 rue Porte de Laure, T04 90 96 11 89, lecalendal.com.* A friendly hotel, complete with contemporary 'Roman' spa, located steps from Arles's amphitheatre. The on-site restaurant serves lunch in the leafy garden during summer, and Oli Pan, an organic gourmet deli, is just downstairs. Parking €8/day.

🍴 Restaurants

Arles *p82*

€€€€ L'Atelier de Jean-Luc Rabanel, *7 rue des Carmes, T04 90 91 07 69, rabanel. com. Wed-Sun 1200-1330 and 2000-2100.* Exquisite double Michelin-starred cuisine, mostly centred around seasonal vegetables; no ordering à la carte allowed. The two daily set menus – seven (€55, €100 with wine) or 13 (€95, €160 with wine) small courses each – are pricey, but so totally unique they're worth it. Next door, Rabanel's Bistro A Côté (T04 90 47 61 13, www.bistro-acote.com) dishes up more traditional Provençal fare.

€€€-€€ Le Galoubet, *18 rue du Docteur Fanton, T04 90 93 18 11. Daily 1200-1500 and 1900-2300.* Long a local favourite, this spot's Mediterranean menu is market-fresh and seasonal. Try grilled aubergine with Parmesan shavings, or *côte de bœuf* with chanterelle mushroom sauce. Two-course lunches are €18, and there's a shady summer terrace for dining out front.

€ Cuisine de Comptoir, *10 rue de la Liberté, T04 90 96 86 28. Mon 1000-2400, Tue-Sat 0830-2400.* Superb little spot grilling up Poilâne loaf tartines (open-faced sandwiches, €9.50-12.50). Each one is served with either a bowl of homemade soup (look out for their tasty carrot and honey) or a salad. A selection of local contemporary art (for sale) is rotated throughout the restaurant's minimalist interior.

Cafés and bars

Comptoir du Sud, *2 rue Jean Jaurès, T04 90 96 22 17. Tue-Fri 1000-1800.* Gourmet sandwiches to eat at the high tables or take away. Try the *sandwich du berger* (€3.50), goat's cheese and fig chutney squeezed between two slices of pistachio bread.

🛍 Shopping

Arles *p82*

You can pick up any of these treats at Arles's weekly **Provençal market** (bd Emile Combes, Sat 0730-1230), at shops in the Old Town or in Saintes-Maries-de-la-Mer: wild rice (grown in Camargue paddies), *saucisson de taureau* (bull salami), absinthe (Van Gogh's tipple of choice), *fleur de sel* (harvested from the Camargue salt marshes), and local olive oil.

🚌 Transport

Arles *p82*

Arles's Old Town is small and easy to walk around. The free **Starlette** shuttle bus runs from the train station to boulevard des Lices, near the tourist office. Taxis can be booked through **Taxi Saliniers** (T04 90 52 22 22, taxi-salinier.com).

The train station is on Avenue Paulin Talabot, T36 35. Ther are frequent trains to Avignon (20-25 mins) and Marseille (55 mins).

The bus station is on Avenue Paulin Talabot, T04 90 49 38 01. Five to six buses daily to Stes-Maries-de-la-Mer (1 hr). Four buses every day July-August, four buses Saturday-Sunday and holidays during June and September, no buses between Arles and Les Baux/St-Remy the rest of the year.

Arles *p82*

Money ATMs throughout the city, including ones around place de la République. **Medical services** **Centre Hospitalier d'Arles**, quart Haut de Fourchon, T04 90 49 29 29. **Pharmacie St Julien**, 25 rue Quatre Septembre, T04 90 96 00 04. **Post office** 5 boulevard des Lices, T36 31. **Tourist information** Boulevard des Lices, T04 90 18 41 20, arlestourisme. com (Apr-Sep daily 0900-1845, Oct Mon-Sat 0900-1745, Sun 1000-1300, Nov-Mar Mon-Sat 0900-1645, Sun 1000-1300). There's also a small tourist office in Arles' train station (Apr-Sep Mon-Fri 0930-1300 and 1400-1800, Oct-Mar 0900-1230 and 1400-1700). Pick up one of the following passes for discounted entry to many of the city's sights: the **Passeport Avantage** (€13.50, €12 students, valid one year) allows access to all of Arles's monuments and museums; the **Passeport Arelate** (€9, €7 students, valid one month) covers free entrance to the Amphithéâtre, Théâtre Antique, the Cryptoportiques, Thermes de Constantin and the Musée Départemental Arles Antique; and the **Passeport Liberté** (€9, €7 students, valid one month) allows the holder entry to five sights (at least one museum, and no more than four monuments). For further information regarding any of Arles's monuments, contact T04 90 49 59 05.

The Camargue

Just north of Arles, the River Rhône splits into two branches – the Grand and Petit Rhônes – before tumbling on into the Mediterranean. The Camargue sweeps southwards: a triangular 930 sq km area of marshland contained between the river's two arms.

One of France's 44 national parks, the Parc Naturel Régional de Camargue is also Western Europe's largest river delta. It's home to vast *étangs* (shallow saline lakes), fresh water reed beds and salt marshes, as well as hundreds of bird species (including flamingos), indigenous bulls and whitish-grey Camargue horses. Dense with wildlife, the area is sparsely populated: Stes-Maries-de-la-Mer, counting less than 2500 permanent residents, is its largest town.

Stes-Maries-de-la-Mer → *For listings, see pages 88-89.*

Named for Ste Marie-Jacobé and Ste Marie-Salomé, who arrived here by boat along with Ste Sara during the first century AD, the tiny town of Stes-Maries-de-la-Mer swells to nearly twenty times its population during the summer months. Nature-lovers base themselves here, striking out on foot, bike and horseback to explore the Camargue's inland lagoons and protected shores.

In town, the prominent Eglise Forteresse pokes above the skyline. Constructed between the ninth and 12th centuries, it houses Ste Sara's statue and relic, surrounded by candles and ex-votos, in its subterranean crypt. Atop the church tower, there's a **terrace** ① *daily 1000-1200 and 1400-sunset, €2, €1.50 child (6-12), under 6s free*, with panoramic views over the Camargue countryside.

Parc Ornithologique de Pont de Gau
① *RD 570, T04 90 97 82 62, parcornithologique.com. Daily Apr-Sep 0900-sunset, Oct-Mar 1000-sunset. €7, €4 child (4-10), under 4s free.*
Set up in 1949 by naturalist André Lamouroux, 16 points of interest mark the 7-km loop around this bird sanctuary; reed-flanked *étangs* and the two observation towers make good vantage points for spying flocks of pink flamingos, plus herons and egrets.

Musée de la Camargue
① *Mas du Pont de Rousty, T04 90 97 10 82, parc-camargue.fr. Apr-Sep Wed-Mon 0900-1230 and 1300-1800, Oct-Mar 1000-1230 and 1300-1700, closed Jan. €4.50, €3 students/over 65, under 18s free.*
On the site of a former sheep farm, the Camargue Museum charts the history of the region, with particular emphasis on local life and communities over the last two centuries. There's

also a 3.5-km Discovery Trail traversing the Mas, taking in fields, crops, marshes and plenty of wildlife.

Salin de Giraud Saltworks

ⓘ *Place Péchiney, T04 42 86 70 20, salins.fr. Ecomuseum: Jul and Aug daily 0930-1230 and 1430-1900, Mar-Jun and Sep-Oct 1015-1215 and 1400-1800, Nov-Feb by appointment only. Free. Tours: Jul-Aug daily 0930, 1100, 1430, 1600 and 1730, Mar-Jun and Sep-Oct daily 1030 and 1530, Nov-Feb by appointment only. €6.80, €5 child (4-13), under 4s free.*

Learn about historical and contemporary salt production methods (it's more fun that it sounds), from the producer of popular French salts La Baleine and Le Saunier de Camargue. Or opt for a one-hour guided tour, via *pétit-train*, of the otherworldly salt marshes, dotted with clouds of pink flamingos.

The Camargue listings

For hotel and restaurant price codes and other relevant information, see pages 10-14.

🛏 Where to stay

Stes-Maries-de-la-Mer *p87*
€€€ Le Pont des Bannes, *Route d'Arles, T04 90 97 80 81 09, pontdesbannes.com.* Between Stes-Maries-de-la-Mer and the Parc Ornithologique de Pont de Gau, these romantic country-style cottages are dotted over islands in the Etang des Massoucles. There's a tasty restaurant on site, as well as an outdoor pool. Breakfast included; discounts possible between October and March.

🍴 Restaurants

Stes-Maries-de-la-Mer *p87*
€€€-€€ Le Bruleur de Loups, *67 av Gilbert Leroy, T04 90 97 83 31, lebruleurdeloups. monsite-orange.fr. Tue 1200-1430, Thu-Mon 1200-1430 and 1930-2230, closed mid Nov-Christmas.* Traditional Camargue cuisine – including a plethora of dishes based around local bull (pavé, côte, filet, terrine and carpaccio) – served up with sea views. The lunch menu is a bargain (€19); evening set menus €23-38.50.

✺ Festivals and events

Stes-Maries-de-la-Mer *p87*
On 24-25 May, Romany gypsies flood into Stes-Maries-de-la-Mer for their patron saint Sara's (also called 'Sara the black') annual feast day. Festivities begin as the statue of Sara is paraded from the church to the sea. The lively procession is repeated on day two with statues of Marie-Jacobé and Marie-Salomé, finishing with a blessing, plus much singing, dancing and celebrations.

◐ What to do

Stes-Maries-de-la-Mer *p87*
Biking
The terrain around Stes-Maries is flat, and well suited to exploration by bike. Rent your wheels at **Le Vélo Saintois** (19 av de la République, T04 90 97 74 56, levelosaintois. camargue.fr, from €15/day). They also hand out free flyers detailing five cycling circuits around the region.

Horse riding
Tamaris, *Route d'Arles, Stes-Maries-de-la-Mer, T04 90 49 67 78, ballades-tamaris. camargue.fr.* Riding for all levels, through the Camargue and on the beach. From €15/hr.

⊖ Transport

Stes-Maries-de-la-Mer *p87*
Five to six buses a day run between Arles and Stes-Maries and take around one hour to get there.

Walking is the best way to get around Stes-Maries once you're there. However, if you need it, Stes-Maries' **Allo Taxi** can be reached on T04 90 97 94 49.

ⓘ Directory

Stes-Maries-de-la-Mer *p87*
Money Place Mireille, next to tourist office, and along avenue d'Arles, both Stes-Maries. **Medical services** Pharmacy on 16 rue Victor Hugo, Stes-Maries, T04 90 97 83 02. **Post office** Avenue Gambetta, Stes-Maries, T36 31. **Tourist information** 5 avenue Van Gogh, Stes-Maries, T04 90 97 82 55, saintesmaries.com (daily Jul-Aug 0900-2000, Apr-Jun and Sep 0900-1900, Mar and Oct 0900-1800, Nov-Feb 0900-1700).

Contents

Background

History

Pre-Christian Provence

Given the Eden-like climatic conditions that prevailed over the area, it's no surprise that the first signs of life started early. The region's fertile valleys were watered by annual snowmelt, warmed by up to 300 days of sun a year and remained relatively sheltered from natural disasters: no Krakatoa or Pompeii-style explosions here. The first human traces were found in the Calanques: cave paintings of hands, bison and horses, which date from up to 27,000 years ago. More settled communities sprang up around 4000 BC, north of here in both the Gorges du Verdon and in the Vallée des Merveilles, where rock art depicts both man and beast.

Marseille's almost perfect harbour came to the attention of Greek traders in around 600 BC; they had stopped here to found the trading post of Massalia. More commercially savvy than their local counterparts, they shipped in vines, nuts and olive trees, all of which would come to thrive in the region. Trade with a nascent Rome grew, especially in wine, encouraging Marseille to ally itself with the expanding might of its partner to the south. Other natural harbours to the east were colonized with Roman commerce in mind, not least Antibes and Nice, founded as 'Nikaia' to commemorate Greek victory over neighbouring Ligurian tribes. In the west, the home port of Marseille backed a winner, supporting Rome's battles with the Carthaginians of Spain, which concluded with the Third Punic war in 146 BC.

Post-victory, the Romans needed a secure route to their new Iberian empire. The Via Domitia was constructed in 118 BC and ran through Gap, Apt, Cavaillon and St-Rémy-de-Provence towards Spain, with feeding and rest stations a day's journey apart. The Germanic tribes of the Teutones and Ambrones were finally mopped up in 102 BC at the Battle of Aquae Sextiae, where the Romans stayed put and founded Aix-en-Provence. It became a constituent part of the Roman Empire, known as Provincia, with surrounding city-states paying tribute or collaborating with the settlers.

But wealthy Marseille blew the peace, favouring Pompey's claim to the Roman Empire over that of Julius Caesar. No prizes for guessing what happened next. Besieged and humiliated, Marseille's assets were given to various Roman colonies including Arles, which was linked directly to Rome with the Via Aurelia. The Via Agrippa, constructed in the decades before Christ, connected Arles to Orange and Avignon. Under the protection of Pax Romana, Provence was left to build the amphitheatres and baths that scatter the region today.

Provence divided and rebuilt

Christianity arrived in Provence around the fourth century AD. St Honoratus disembarked on the Iles de Lérins to create his monastery in AD 410, while the Abbey of St Victor in Marseille was founded five years later. But when Rome and its Christian state religion fell in the late fifth century, an alien crowd of Goths, Visigoths, Burgundians and Franks poured into Provence. As in much of Europe, both the authority and aqueducts of the Roman Empire collapsed, and famine and pestilence were widespread. Muslim Saracens controlled the sea.

As the ports of coastal Provence fell into decline, the region looked inland for its wealth. The Carolingian dynasty brought in a period of continuity and peace, not least under the wonderfully named Pepin the Short, who drove the Saracens out of Gaul. Agriculture developed further under his son, Charlemagne, who reunited the Western Roman Empire. But squabbles broke out over his inheritance and the empire disintegrated a generation later, leaving the interior open to Norman invasion and the coast to renewed Saracen attack, the latter occupying Ramatuelle, St-Tropez and other strategic towns in the Massif des Maures.

After a century of pillaging, locals tired of their Muslim guests and united under Count William of Arles. Following a series of skirmishes, the local forces finally beat the Saracens at the Battle of Tourtour near La Garde-Freinet in AD 973, setting in stone the victor's reign as William 1st of Provence.

William's death heralded dynastic disagreements, which once again plagued the region. Provence was subsumed into the Holy Roman Empire in 1032, with the westernmost part governed by the Catalans. But this loose Christian overlordship brought more harmony to the area than was usual, and a great programme of building was embarked upon: Aix Cathedral and the St-Trophime church in Arles date from this time, as do the Sénanque abbey near Gordes and Chartreuse de la Verne near Collobrières. The Provençal language spread, carried throughout the region by travelling Troubadour poets. The daughter of the last Count of Provence Raymond Bérenger IV tied the knot with Charles d'Anjou, brother of the French king Louis IX, ushering in 250 years of Angevin rule.

Meanwhile, as the maritime trading powers of Pisa and Genoa grew, so did their influence along the Provence coast. While the relocation of the Papacy to Avignon for a 60-year sojourn in 1309 went on to cultivate further cultural and trade links.

French takeover

Having lost the Kingdom of Naples in 1441, Angevin control of Provence was on its last legs when its ruler, 'Good King' René of Anjou, died in Aix in 1480. Governorship passed to his nephew, Charles, who died childless the following year. The inheritance then passed to Charles' cousin, Louis XI of France, whose nickname 'the Universal Spider' more than gently hints at his scheming, manipulative ways.

Louis took a sledgehammer to the subtle knot of local government. Toulon was razed and Provençal governors were forcibly replaced with French ones. The 'Act of Union' with France in 1486 was little more than a hostile incorporation of the southern province. The Ordinance of Villers-Cotterêts in 1539 decreed that all baptisms, deaths and marriages must be notarised, and that all must be done so in French, sealing the fate of Latin, Provençal and many other minority tongues. The country became even more united in the face of a common enemy during the 16th century wars with Italy, which led to the fortification of Marseille and Toulon.

But once again, Provence's enemy came from within. The spread of Calvinism throughout the region in the 1550s, most notably in Orange and the Lubéron, put these 'Huguenots' on a collision course with the staunchly Catholic former Papal lands around Avignon. The Wars of Religion slowed with Henry IV's Edict of Nantes in 1598, which guaranteed freedom of worship for both Protestants and Catholics, but not before decades of terrible atrocities from both sides. The rule of Louis XIII, aided by the crafty Cardinal Richelieu from 1624, ushered in a more peaceful balance together with a fortification programme along the Provence coast. Louis's childless wife of 23 years, Anne of Austria, visited Contignac in 1638 to pray for a son. Sadly, the new arrival may not have been what she wished for. That September, the over-confident fop Louis XIV, aka The Sun King, was unleashed on to the world.

In 72 years of eccentric reign, Louis cared little for Provence. Nevertheless, he still managed to send it into turmoil by repealing the Edict of Nantes, turning Marseille's guns on itself and converting the Chateau d'If into an Alcatraz-style prison for reactionaries. The Black Death paid a visit to Marseille in 1720, killing up to 100,000 people in the area. Back in Versailles, Louis XV fared little better than his great-grandfather. One feels sorry for poor Louis XVI, who was landed with the inheritance of a poverty-ridden powder keg in 1775; he ended up marrying Marie Antoinette then losing his head in 1793.

As revolution swept France, the dockyards of Marseille were up in arms and religious buildings all over the region were requisitioned. Churches in La Garde-Freinet even took to hiding their bells lest they be trashed by revolutionaries. Toulon was occupied by a pro-Royalist British fleet in 1793, and only the dogged determination of a young artillery officer, Napoleon Bonaparte, saw them on their way. An older, but no less confident, Napoleon returned from his exile on Elba to the beaches of Golfe-Juan in 1815 to begin his march to Paris via Grasse, Entrevaux and Digne. The restoration of the Bourbons after French disaster at Waterloo (personified by the originally-named Louis XVIII) did little to soothe the anti-royalist passions of the south.

With revolutions and coups in 1848 and 1851, it wasn't until the mid-1800s that Provence finally calmed down. As trade with France's new colonies in Algeria and the Far East expanded, so again did the southern ports and their hinterland. A rail link to Marseille and the upgrading of its harbour for steamships saw the city boom. French ruler Napoleon III helped the reunifying Italians defeat France's traditional enemy, the Austrians, during the Austro-Sardinian wars in 1859. The Duchy of Nice was added to Provence in the bargain. With the arrival of the Train Bleu to Nice in 1864, the entire region of Provence was finally considered safe enough for wealthy British aristocrats, led by Queen Victoria, to begin wintering here.

Foreign invasion

A thousand minor nobles imitated the major royals. Spending the winter in Hyères or Nice's Cimiez became the thing to do. Further west, there was an artistic exodus to St-Tropez, Cassis and L'Estaque by the likes of Cézanne, Signac, Matisse, Bonnard, Renoir and Dufy. Conscription for World War I decimated the local population, but the celebrities (including Coco Chanel) and tourists flocked to the Provençal coast for a dose of unbridled liberalism in the interwar years, or *les années folles*. These well-heeled foreigners were joined by regular Frenchmen, enjoying a paid state holiday for the first time in 1936. But in the distance, the drums of World War II were already beating the time.

France surrendered six weeks after hostilities began in mid-1940, when the allegedly impregnable Maginot Line near St-Agnès collapsed. Italian soldiers occupied the Riviera as some of its celebrity residents, including Somerset Maugham, were evacuated by coal barge. While the Italians proved a light touch, patently ignoring calls to round up Provence's Jewish population, the collaborationist Vichy regime, which ruled the non-German occupied part of southern France, did not. Thousands were deported to concentration camps in Germany and Poland, although many Jewish children found refuge in Monaco.

As the Germans formally occupied Provence in late 1942, many locals were driven to the resistance. The communist party, with its heartlands in the docks of Marseille and Toulon,

Artists in Provence

Provence's quality of light, combined with the intensity of its coastal and countryside colours, has long acted as an irresistible magnet for artists. Claude Monet may have dipped his toes off the shores off the French Riviera's shores in the late 1880s, but it was Vincent Van Gogh, Paul Gauguin and Paul Cézanne who truly earmarked Provence as a place of modern art pilgrimage.

Van Gogh arrived in the South of France in 1888. During the final two years of his life, the artist painted with a prolific intensity, turning his attention first to colourful Arles, depicting all its vigorous vibrancy. Like Impressionists before him, Van Gogh focused less on replicating what he saw; he instead channelled his creativity into use of colour and bold strokes, getting an image's personal effect onto canvas. These methods, and their results, were rarely embraced and frequently abhorred, emotions that played on Van Gogh's fragile mental stability.

Fellow artist and friend Paul Gauguin soon joined Van Gogh in Arles for a period of two all-consuming months. Together they painted Van Gogh's yellow house, the Roman necropolis of Les Alyscamps (see page 84), the *Night Café* and each other. But they were both toeing their own abyss of depression, and frequently fought. One quarrel ended with Van Gogh taking a razor to his ear, landing him in the Hospital Hôtel-Dieu (now Espace Van Gogh, see page 83).

The Dutchman soon left both Gauguin and Arles in favour of the Monastère Saint-Paul de Mausole (see page 79) in Saint-Rémy-de-Provence. Staying at the monastery for over a year, Van Gogh created an incredible 143 paintings, including his famous *Starry Night and The Olive Trees*, before abandoning the south altogether.

---

was a chief player in the movement. Toulon suffered a double blow during the war: the French fleet was scuttled by its commanders before it could fall into German hands, then the town was blown to bits a few months later as Allied bombs hit Nazi positions in the bay. General Patch led the Allied army landings on the beaches of St-Tropez in 1944 and headed for Manosque and Gap, while General Vigier of the Free French Forces liberated Avignon and Arles.

Provence's post-war recovery was sluggish. Blocky, stocky buildings took the place of bombed-out residences in the larger cities. Yet more flats shot up to house the migrants from France's Asian, African and Maghreb ex-colonies, not least the *pieds noirs* from Algeria, a million of whom were left homeless after the French withdrawal in 1962. Both state and US Marshall Plan aid got the region moving again, but these handouts combined with a slow pace of success bred corruption, particularly along the coast. But with grand projects like the Paris-Marseille *autoroute* in 1970, the Paris-Aix TGV line in 2001 and, most recently, Marseille's revolutionary Euroméditerranée project, due for completion in 2013, things are looking up. The final foreign invasion – this time of sun-seeking tourists – has been heartily welcomed by the locals in most cases. After 27,000 years of action, they could probably do with a holiday too.

Contents

Footnotes

Menu reader

General

petit déjeuner breakfast

déjeuner lunch (restaurants generally serve between 1200 and 1430).

dîner dinner or supper (restaurants serve dinner from 1900-2200; in rural towns it may be difficult to find a restaurant open after 2100).

hors d'œuvre appetisers, many restaurants also offer little *amuse-gueules* or *amuse-bouches* – literally throat- or mouth-teasers – after you've ordered.

entrées starters

les plats main courses

plat principal main course

menu / formule set menu

plat du jour dish of the day

à la carte individually-priced menu items

carte des vins wine list

une carafe d'eau a carafe of water

fait(e) maison home-made

Appellation d'Origine Contrôlée (AOC) label of regulated origin, signifying quality; usually associated with wine, though can also apply to regional foods such as cheeses.

Label Rouge often applied to poultry, label indicates premium quality and standards in production.

Agriculture Biologique (AB) organically produced product

biologique or *bio* organic

Drinks (*boissons*)

apéritif drink taken before dinner.

digestif after-dinner drink, usually a liqueur or spirit.

eau gazeuse / pétillante sparkling / slightly sparkling mineral water.

eau plate / minérale still / mineral water

bouteille bottle

dégustation tasting

un verre de… a glass of…

un (verre de) vin rouge / blanc / rosé… a glass of red / white / rosé wine.

pichet jug, used to serve water, wine or cider.

sec dry

demi-sec medium dry – or slightly sweet when referring to champagne.

doux the sweetest champagne or cider

kir popular apéritif made with white wine and a fruit liqueur – blackcurrant (*cassis*) is popular.

petit(e) small

grand(e) big, large

pression a glass of draught beer

une bière a beer

demi small beer (33cl)

cidre cider

panaché beer/lemonade shandy

pastis anise-flavoured apéritif from around Marseille

jus de fruit fruit juice. Bars usually have a wide variety of flavours of bottled fruit juice.

orange pressée freshly-squeezed orange juice.

sirop fruit syrup or cordial served mixed with water, sparkling water or soda. Popular flavours are *grenadine* (pomegranate), *menthe* (mint) or *citron* (lemon).

diabolo menthe refreshing green drink made with mint syrup mixed with lemonade.

un coca Coca-Cola

glaçons ice cubes

café coffee (black espresso)

un (grand) crème a (large) white coffee

une noisette espresso with a dash of milk

chocolat chaud hot chocolate, can be too sweet for some tastes. Chocolatiers will serve the best quality chocolate, and you can sweeten to taste.

lait milk

un thé tea, usually served nature with a slice of lemon (*au citron*) – if you want milk ask for *un peu de lait froid*, a little cold milk.

une tisane / infusion herbal tea: *tisane de menthe* (mint tea), *tisane de camomille* (camomile tea) and *tisane de tilleul* (lime blossom) are the most popular.

Fruit (*fruits*) and vegetables (*légumes*)

ail garlic

ananas pineapple

artichaut artichoke

asperge asparagus

blettes Swiss chard

cassis blackcurrants

céleri-rave celeriac, usually served grated in mayonnaise.

cèpes porcini mushrooms

champignons de Paris button mushrooms

châtaignes chestnuts

choux cabbage

citron lemon

citrouille or *potiron* pumpkin

cocos small, white beans

courge marrow or squash

épinards spinach

fenouil fennel

fèves broad beans

figues figs

figues de Barbarie prickly pears

fraises strawberries

framboises raspberries

gratin dauphinois a popular side-dish of potato slices layered with cream, garlic and butter and baked in the oven.

haricots verts green beans, often served as an accompaniment to a main course.

lentilles vertes green lentils

mesclun a mixture of young salad leaves.

mirabelles small golden plums

myrtilles blueberries

noix walnuts

oseille sorrel, often served in a sauce with salmon.

pêches peaches

petits pois peas
poireaux leeks
poires pears
pomme de terre potato, primeurs are new potatoes, and frites are chips (chips being crisps).
pommes apples, the Reinette d'Orléans and Reine des Reinettes are local varieties.
prunes plums
ratatouille summer vegetables cooked in a tomato and garlic sauce.
soupe au pistou a spring vegetable soup with pistou.
truffe truffle

Meat (*viande*) and poultry (*volaille*)

agneau lamb
andouillette soft sausage made from pig's small intestines, usually grilled.
au point medium cooked meat (or tuna steak), usually still pink inside.
bien cuit well-cooked
blanquette de veau veal stew in white sauce with cream, vegetables and mushrooms.
bleu barely-cooked meat, almost raw.
bœuf beef
boucherie butcher's shop or display
canard duck
charcuterie encompasses sausages, hams and cured or salted meats.
chevreuil venison, roe deer
confit process to preserve meat, usually duck, goose or pork (e.g. confit de canard).
cuisse de grenouille frog's leg
daube marinated and slow-cooked beef, lamb or bull, vegetable and red wine stew; also used to fill pasta in the south of France.
dinde turkey
escalope thin, boneless slice of meat.
faux-filet beef sirloin
foie-gras fattened goose or duck liver.
fumé(e) smoked
géline de Touraine or la Dame-Noire grain-fed chicken prized by restaurateurs, awarded a Label Rouge.
gigot d'agneau leg of lamb
jambon ham; look for jambon d'Amboise, an especially fine ham.
lapin rabbit
médaillon small, round cut of meat or fish.
mouton mutton
pavé thickly cut steak
pieds et paquets tripe stuffed with pork, traditionally served with lambs' feet, a speciality of Marseille.
pintade guinea-fowl
porc pork
pot-au-feu slow-cooked beef and vegetable stew.
poulet chicken
rillettes a coarse pork pâté.

rillons big chunks of pork cooked in pork fat.
ris de veau sweetbreads
sanglier wild boar
saucisse small sausage
saucisson salami, eaten cold
saucisson sec air-dried salami
veau veal
taureau bull

Fish (*poisson*) and seafood (*fruits de mer*)

aiglefin haddock
anchoïade anchovy-based spread
anchois anchovies
anguille eel
bouillabaisse Marseillaise traditional fish stew from Marseille, served in two courses (first the soup, then the fish).
boulots sea snails
bourride white fish stew, thickened with aïoli.
brochet pike
cabillaud cod
calamar squid
coquillage shellfish
colin hake
crevettes prawns
dorade sea bream
homard lobster
huîtres oysters
lotte monkfish
loup de mer sea bass
morue salt-cod
moules mussels
oursins sea urchins
palourdes clams
poissons de rivière river fish
poulpe octopus
poutine very tiny, young sardines, most often cooked in an omelette or served raw.
rascasse scorpion fish
rouget red mullet
Saint-Pierre John Dory
sardines sardines
saumon salmon
soupe de poisson a smooth rockfish-based soup, served with croutons, rouille and grated gruyère cheese.
soupions small squid
thon tuna
truite trout

Desserts (*desserts*)

chantilly whipped, sweetened cream
chichi fregi deep-fried, orange-blossom doughnuts from L'Estaque.
clafoutis a fruit tart (usually cherries) covered in a custard-style filling, served hot or cold
compôte stewed fruit, often as a purée.

crème anglaise thin custard; unlike English custard, it is normally served cold.

crème brûlée chilled custard cream dessert with a caramelised top.

crème caramel baked custard flavoured with caramel.

fromage blanc unsweetened dairy product with a refreshing flavour served on its own or offered with a fruit coulis – most people add a little sugar.

glace ice cream

boules de glace scoops of ice cream

coupe glacée cold dessert with ice cream, fruit or nuts, chocolate or chantilly.

le parfum flavour, only when referring to ice cream or yoghurt.

île flottante soft meringue floating on custard, topped with caramel sauce.

liègeois chilled chocolate or coffee ice cream-based dessert topped with chantilly.

navettes orange-blossom biscuits from Marseille.

pâtisserie pastries, cakes and tarts – also the place where

they are sold.

sabayon creamy dessert made with beaten eggs, sugar and wine or liqueur.

tarte au citron lemon tart, ubiquitous around Menton during winter.

tarte Tatin upside-down apple tart

tourte de blettes sweet, Swiss chard tart from Nice.

Other

aïoli garlic mayonnaise

assiette plate (e.g. *assiette de charcuterie*)

Béarnaise sauce made of a wine reduction with tarragon, shallots and chervil, served hot with grilled beef or fish.

bagna càuda raw vegetables served with a hot garlic, olive oil and anchovy dip, popular throughout the Alps.

beurre butter

beurre blanc buttery white wine sauce often served with fish.

Bordelaise red wine sauce served with steak.

boulangerie bakery selling bread and viennoiserie.

brioche a soft, sweet bread made with eggs and butter.

casse-croûte literally 'to break a crust' – a snack.

crêpe large pancake served with various fillings as a dessert or snack.

croque-monsieur grilled ham and cheese sandwich.

croque-madame as above but topped with a fried egg.

croissant rich and flaky crescent-shaped roll usually served at breakfast.

crudités raw vegetables served sliced or diced with a dressing, as a starter or sandwich filling.

en croûte literally 'in crust'; food cooked in a pastry parcel.

escargots snails

fleur de sel speciality salt collected by hand, particularly from the Camargue.

forestière generally sautéed with mushrooms.

fougasse a type of Provençal bread, plain or filled with mushrooms, tomatoes, aubergine or Roquefort.

fromage cheese

fromage de chèvre goat's milk cheese

fromage de brebis ewe's milk cheese

galette savoury filled pancake made with buckwheat flour, served as a starter or main course.

garniture garnish, side-dish

gâteau cake

gaufre waffle, usually served with chocolate sauce

Hollandaise rich oil and egg yolk sauce flavoured with lemon juice

œuf egg

pain bread – choose from a rich variety of flavoured breads as well as the traditional baguette.

pain au chocolat similar to a croissant, but pillow shaped and filled with chocolate.

pan bagnat sandwich version of salade niçoise, dressed with lashings of olive oil and vinegar.

pâte pastry or dough, not to be confused with *pâtes*, which is pasta or *pâté*, the meat terrine

petits farcis usually small onions, tomatoes, peppers and courgettes stuffed with a mix of veal, Parmesan and vegetables.

pissaladière Niçois onion tart, usually eaten as a snack.

pistou a basil and garlic sauce, similar to Italian pesto but without pine nuts or Parmesan.

riz rice

rouille saffron, garlic and paprika mayonnaise, served with soupe de poisson and bouillabaisse.

salade niçoise salad usually made up of tomatoes, peppers, artichokes, boiled egg, olives, tinned tuna or anchovies; may also include potatoes and green beans.

salade verte green salad with vinaigrette dressing.

socca savoury chickpea flour pancake from Nice.

soupe/potage soup

viennoiserie baked items such as *croissants* and *brioches*.

tapenade Provençal olive, caper and anchovy spread.

Useful phrases

I'd like to reserve a table *Je voudrais réserver une table*

For two people at 2000 *Pour deux personnes, à vingt heures*

What do you recommend? *Qu'est-ce que vous me conseillez?*

I'd like the set menu please *Je vais prendre le menu / la formule s'il vous plait*

Does it come with salad? *Est-ce que c'est servi avec de la salade?*

I'd like something to drink *Je voudrais quelque chose à boire*

I'm a vegetarian *Je suis végétarien / végétarienne*

I don't eat… *Je ne mange pas de…*

Where are the toilets? *Où sont les toilettes?*

The bill, please *L'addition, s'il vous plait*

Index → *Entries in bold refer to maps.*